Praise for *The Imprint Jo*

"Liliane demonstrates that the imprints of our past need ... Sharing her years of personal and professional experiences in recovery and counseling, Liliane shows how lives can be transformed, and provides the reader with tools to begin their personal transformational journey. This is a must read for anyone wishing to take their inner lives to higher levels of greatness, and for any professional looking for a transformational resource to use with their clients in all forms of healing and recovery."

> Donna Mailloux, Psychologist, Researcher, and Adjunct Professor,
> Carleton University, Ottawa

"There has never been any doubt in my mind that we are all products of our environment as well as of our genetics. And both of those factors, whether we like it or not, lead us to some rather peculiar behavioral patterns or, probably even more accurately, the repeating patterns of such behavior. What has never been quite clear to me though was exactly why and how we keep repeating such actions, which are all too oftentimes very destructive and/or self-destructive. The best answer I've found so far is the one provided by Liliane Desjardins in her book *The Imprint Journey*. Never judgmental, never preachy and never overly technical, this is one of those rare books that will make you think and re-evaluate who you are and why you are acting the way you are. If you are lucky, you will gather enough courage to deal with the issues that bother you. All the tools are there, you just need to find the courage to make that first step."

> Olivera Baumgartner-Jackson, *Reader Views*

"In *The Imprint Journey*, Liliane Desjardins has boldly stepped forward to tell her own story of dysfunction, misguided beliefs, and an amazing recovery. After working for more than thirty years as a clinical addiction specialist, formulating the Desjardins Unified Model of Treatment of Addictions, co-founding *Pavillon*, and penning *Rewriting Life Scripts*, she now tells her own long overdue story of an amazing journey that transformed her into a woman with a mission to help others find their authentic selves. Liliane's personal story reads like a good novel, full of excitement as well as fear and confusion, that reveals to the reader how she formed her often negative imprints—misguided beliefs that crippled and limited her life

The Imprint Journey is a book that will help inspire and transform anyone wise enough to read it. Even people who have been in recovery for many years will find new insights into themselves in these pages that will help them live even more authentic lives. Thank you, Liliane, for telling your story—for having the courage to share so much of yourself with others, and for leaving this book as part of your legacy and the culmination of an unforgettably powerful life and career."

> Tyler R. Tichelaar, Ph.D.,
> author of the award-winning novel *Narrow Lives*

"*The Imprint Journey* will touch your very soul and make way for profound transformation. From personal story to practical steps, Liliane walks with her readers on the path of awakening. Your life will be changed. It is in understanding our imprints that we open to the desires of our heart's. No longer does our past have to play out in the 'now', or in the future. No longer does our past have to sabotage our soul's longing. Take a walk on the healing side of life and get ready for your Greatness and be transformed!"

Carolyn Craft, Psychotherapist, Broadcaster, Unity Minister
"Waking Up With Carolyn Craft" – Sirius Satellite Radio

"Mrs. Desjardins has written a book that's well-beyond interesting. With masterful presentation, the first section is an amazing story dedicated to her childhood; in fact, it reads almost as if it were an extremely well-written historical novel about WWII. The second half of this fascinating work actually explains and outlines Mrs. Desjardins' work that she's been immersed in for over thirty years; a work that, I believe, could help a great many people change the course of their lives.

Whether you're in recovery of some sort, or you find yourself in a monumental depression, the way this author tells you about how you got there, and how she describes the fact that your Authentic Self is your real self buried under all the negative garbage you bear witness to every day, is a new and fresh idea that will help many people who are desperately trying to find the sun in their dark, dismal world.

Not only can this book be categorized under informative and interesting, but it is also a truly inspirational, uplifting story about how one woman found a way to offer herself forgiveness, at the same time finding a way to be grateful for every aspect of her life, and granting herself the freedom to live it."

Amy Lignor, *Feathered Quill Book Reviews*

"In this honest, inspiring and definitive book, Liliane Desjardins leads us on a path of self-discovery and hope. The bridge built as her life's work and shared in these lucid and powerful pages, connects us to deep and sustained healing, renewed vision and the kind of peace that is our spiritual birthright!"

Rev. Steve Bolen, Sr. Minister
Unity Church of the Hills, Austin, TX

"I consider Liliane Desjardin's *The Imprint Journey* to be a must read for anyone who is interested in changing, or helping others to change, some aspect of their lives. She brings true insight and sensitivity to the field of personal growth, It is a book that will serve as a workbook and be used again and again."

Joel Carroll, M.D.

The Imprint Journey

A Path of Lasting Transformation Into Your Authentic Self

Liliane Desjardins

Foreword by Douglas Ziedonis, MD, MPH

Life Scripts Press

Library of Congress Cataloging-in-Publication Data

Desjardins, Liliane, 1938-
    The imprint journey : a path of lasting transformation into your authentic self /
Liliane Desjardins ; foreword by Douglas Ziedonis.
        p. cm. -- (Life scripts recovery series)
    Includes index.
    ISBN-13: 978-1-61599-087-0 (trade paper : alk. paper)
    ISBN-10: 1-61599-087-9 (trade paper : alk. paper)
    ISBN-13: 978-1-61599-088-7 (hardcover : alk. paper)
    ISBN-10: 1-61599-088-7 (hardcover : alk. paper)
    1. Desjardins, Liliane, 1938- 2. Recovering addicts--Croatia--Biography. 3.
Dependency (Psychology) 4. Awareness. I. Title.
    HV5805.D46A3 2011
    362.29092--dc22
    [B]
                                         2010048729

    Distributed by Ingram Book Group (USA/CAN), New Leaf Distributing,
Bertram's Books (UK), Agapea (Spain), The Hachette Group (France), Angus &
Robertson (Australia).

    Published by Life Scripts Press, an imprint of
Loving Healing Press   Toll free 888-761-6268
5145 Pontiac Trail   FAX 734-663-6861
Ann Arbor, MI 48105   www.LHPress.com
USA   info@LHPress.com

Contents

This book is dedicated to Love

The Power of Love
Love that transforms and heals
Love that creates and builds

To my own grandchildren Emmanuel, Samantha, Francesca, Chantale, and Roxanne, beautiful, wise, courageous bright souls; the shining stars and joy of my life.

To my daughter Caroline, the brilliant woman of the world, the enthusiastic, creative scholar devoted to excellence. The beautiful loving soul whose love healed my heart.

To my son Richard, the bright light of recovery. The courageous, committed, and brilliant teacher, the bold and daring heart of service. To my loyal son who is my teacher of integrity.

Yes to my beloved children, the free inspiring spirits making a difference in this world.

To Vivianne my stepdaughter, whose love for her children and husband continues to be an inspiration. The brave woman who re-wrote the script of family dynamics.

To my daughter-in-law Gina, beautiful, warm, devoted, creative, compassionate soul, a woman in whose presence one feels safe and loved.

To my sons-in-law Joseph and Douglas, whose goodness of heart and love of family is a never ending inspiration. With their sense of humor they light up a home.

This book is dedicated to my husband Gilles. The man with a vision of Wholeness and Transformation. The man whose unconditional love heals and transforms. The Pioneer and builder of dreams, whose daring spirit, set high the bar of transformational recovery. The love of my life without whom this book would be just an idea. To my best friend whose unwavering faith reinforces mine.

To Nana, my step-mom, whose spirit of survival carried us all through the storms of life.

And to all who have walked with me on the Path of Recovery and Transformation.

Acknowledgments

I am grateful to so many people in my life who were and are a vital part of this book. My gratitude goes to Irene Watson, my writing mentor, my Master Mind partner, and my friend. Thank you for your vision, love, and guidance that gave me wings to fly.

To Tyler Tichelaar, my editor. I will be forever grateful for your trust, your refined talent, and professionalism, your patience with my hesitations, your warm and caring spirit, and your understanding of the vision. Thank you, Tyler.

My gratitude goes to Dr. Douglas Ziedonis, the brilliant scientific mind with a heart of gold, whose guidance and friendship through the years has been such a treasure. You have inspired me to be the recovery bridge between spirituality and science.

Thank you to my publisher, Victor R Volkman; he's my wonderful publisher and friend, whom I have never seen in person but fully trust.

I am so grateful to all the bold and daring souls whose stories of pain and triumphs give vibrancy to this book. I know how busy you are; thank you for taking the time to help this world be a better place.

My deep gratitude goes to my sponsors Jeannine Prevost and Jack Boland and to my teacher Rev. Michael B. Beckwith. They have shaped my faith and imprinted my new belief system.

Thank you to Patty Murphy and Dale Hole for their trust and support of our mission; without them the mission would not have been the same.

Thank you to Chuck Hayes and Robin Britt for understanding the value and vision of our model. Thank you for your boldness and tenacity.

Thank you to all staff members from Canada and North Carolina, as well as all the volunteers. Your spirit of health, wholeness, and transformation has made a difference in this world.

Thank you to all my faithful friends, prayer partners, and fellows in recovery. You were and are the wind beneath my wings.

And last but not least, I am truly grateful for the spirit of innocence, joy, and playful energy our little dog Angel gives me daily. Thank you, Angel, for your unconditional love in the early hours of the mornings when this book was being written.

Foreword

Ever feel like you are walking through life on autopilot and making the same choices over and over? Our brain can get stuck in repeat mode, which limits our options and potential. Increasing our awareness and better understanding our brain's "imprints" can be the first steps to healing and transformation.

We all have the capability to be more present in the moment—more fully aware of where and who we are. What distracts us? Where is our mind spinning? Is our mind fear-based and over-focused on the future? Or perhaps we are concerned and ruminate about past events? Where does our inner wisdom come from? What shapes our values and beliefs? Imprints! They began with the genetic code we were given at the moment of conception and developed through the many events, experiences, messages, and moments along our journey. These imprints influence our relationships with others, self, and God. They shape our behaviors, expectations, and perceptions. However, with new awareness and understanding, they can be changed.

In *The Imprint Journey: A Path of Lasting Transformation Into Your Authentic Self*, Liliane Desjardins shares her own journey and lessons learned as a therapist in an intimate and humble manner that is insightful, clear, and concise. Her book provides a fresh perspective on pursuing mindfulness and personal transformation. She reminds us that we have "hidden treasures" in our "true identity" and "authentic self" that can be overshadowed by life's pains and fears.

Liliane's book reflects her more than thirty years of clinical experience using the Desjardins Unified Model for treating substance and process addictions. Her work has been built on a strong foundation of traditional therapy with new insights from her clinical and personal experience. She can blend the Desjardins model well with traditional therapy approaches.

The author speaks to us as both a friend and as an experienced therapist, raising useful questions for reflection that will help us better appreciate our imprints and their effect on our thinking, beliefs, perceptions, expectations, and even on our physiological responses to external events. This book will help anyone who desires to transform his or her life through the exploration of imprints. You might read it in one sitting, but you are likely to go back to it many times as you have new ideas, challenges, and experiences.

I have known Liliane and her work for over fifteen years, and I have seen her in action as an amazing clinician who has helped thousands of individuals transform their lives, finding their authentic self with increased awareness, acceptance, and gratitude. From my own conversations with Liliane, I have been inspired and helped to develop into a more effective clinician and person.

As a physician and psychiatrist, I have worked with many individuals, couples, and families who suffer from addiction, mental illness, grief, separation, and other life stressors. The wisdom in this book could be a valuable resource and source of support to all of them as a self-help guide or tool in therapy or a support group. As a leader and teacher at the University of Massachusetts Medical School and UMass Memorial Health Care system (as well as at UCLA, Yale, and Rutgers in the past), I know that students, staff, and faculty benefit from having time for self-reflection and from help with balancing work, family, friends, and community. Increasing awareness, one of the most important things we can all do, is the first step in Liliane's model.

Liliane's transformational guide is grounded in deep healing traditions and also resonates well with modern neuroscience and the cutting edge science of "epigenetics." Recent neuroscience breakthroughs are helping us to understand better how our imprints affect our ability to be aware and transform our lives. For example, our research team at UMass is studying awareness and other key phenomena involved in healing and recovery through the windows of brain imaging and genetic research. Scientists now understand that the genetic material we receive from our parents can be altered and changed in a healthy or less healthy direction due to exposure to physical forces (such as chemicals, addictive drugs, therapeutic touch, and medications) and powerful emotional experiences (such as war, emotional abuse, love, and positive therapy experiences). Encoded through our brain's memory pathways, the imprints of our life's experiences impact all our thinking, feeling, and doing. These changes have a biological basis, but transformation is more than just biology—it is spiritual and encompasses all aspects of being human.

Liliane's book demonstrates the power of personal narrative—the power of authenticity and sharing your experiences to give others strength and hope. Through her and others' personal stories in this book, we can reflect on how our imprints ripple through our lives. During the first part of the book (Chapters 1-7), we connect with Liliane's story as a model for how we can reflect on our own imprints and how they have shaped our perceptions, beliefs, and actions.

Imprints that have affected my own life include a core identity influenced by immigration, acculturation, and assimilation into America. Being a first generation Latvian-American whose parents fled as adolescents from their homeland of Latvia during World War II, I can connect with Liliane's reflections on her own immigration experience and her journey through war, oppression, and forced migration while trying to maintain a culture and core values. Such events can alter our fundamental view of the world: What's real? Who do you trust? Trauma, disconnection, uncertainty, isolation, and fear can leave their imprint for several generations and cause ripples of post-traumatic stress, dissociation, denial, and minimization of reality. These events can also lead to transformative experiences and new opportunities. For example, despite the heavy imprints of war's traumas, my own parents were able to cope and, through hope, evolve to achieve healthy, spiritual, and productive lives.

Part II of the book turns from Liliane's own story to provide "Tools for Your Imprint Journey." Its mission is to help us uncover the core components of our imprints (Chapter 9), including considering the genetic, familial, societal, cultural, and religious influences. Imprints impact how we perceive, act, and think about love, relationships, family, health, finances, religion, education, social activities, life's purpose, and our sense of accomplishment. Chapter 10, a particularly important chapter, helps us uncover positive imprints—hidden treasures and sources of strength from our parents and other sources. Chapter 11 focuses on our spiritual energy's healing power and shows how it is linked to our capacity for empowerment and transformation. In Chapter 15, this energy or awakening helps us to access our authentic self through awareness, forgiveness, cognitive shifting, gratitude, acceptance, and other important steps in transformation. This core chapter is at the heart of the theory behind Liliane's approach. Her nine core action steps to transformation are awareness, admittance, release, willingness to change, forgiveness, gratitude, meditation and affirmations, enhancing consciousness, and acceptance of love.

Liliane's steps to transformation provide a guide to the journey of transformation and freedom from perceived limitations based on our imprints. Not only does she describe the steps; she offers terrific questions for reflection and goals, strategies, and techniques. For example, she describes the helpful technique of a "Gratitude List" that will help us appreciate what we receive from others. Another example is the use of meditation, including visualization and affirmations. Meditation is a universal way to cultivate awareness, and Liliane respects the contemplative traditions and expands these approaches with other models. Throughout, she offers wisdom, values, and hope. From my own experience reading these steps, I could imagine some readers will follow each step one after another and others will want to modify the order of the steps on their journey. The model allows for flexibility and staying true to yourself.

In summary, this book is a wonderful gift from an outstanding therapist. Liliane has put together a story of her life and a guidebook for others that will help us all on our journey. Your life can be enriched by reading and following the steps outlined in this book, as well as by reflecting on the examples and questions it offers. I am honored to be able to make a very small contribution to this book, and I am grateful that Liliane has shared both her life's story and her wisdom in the service of helping us all to be more accepting, respectful, and open to our true selves and full potential.

Douglas Ziedonis, MD, MPH
Professor and Chair, Department of Psychiatry
Director, UMass Center of Excellence in Addictions
University of Massachusetts Medical School / UMass Memorial Health Care System

Introduction

We live in a fascinating time of human development. Our planet and mankind are undergoing a lot of changes and experiencing a lot of chaos brought about by that change.

Governing systems and structures are breaking down. Religious fanatics are fighting wars and killing in the name of God. We experience a daily overload of information. Our news media fails to report with journalistic integrity, but rather, it focuses on sensationalism to get the highest ratings.

Our technology has surpassed our humanity. The Internet has changed the planet's entire communication system, bringing the world into our living rooms, while creating islands of human isolation and escape.

For many, love and intimacy have been replaced by cybersex, sex scandals, sex abuse, and child pornography. We are fighting but losing the war on drugs. Now we have legal pushers: greedy doctors, pharmaceutical companies, and an entire out-of-control healthcare system keeping America medicated. We have become a society of addicts craving instant gratification and instant solutions.

Corporate America, with its lack of accountability, lack of ethics, corruption, and greed mirrors back our own immaturity and irresponsibility, making them the agenda of the day that almost collapsed the entire economy.

Our planet is crying for help and responsible stewardship. Global warming, hurricanes and tsunamis, earthquakes and fires, polluted waters, and dying species have become daily dramas.

Yet, it is all so paradoxical. Out of chaos comes the greatest creative growth. Chaos brings order just as light eliminates the darkness.

We are collectively undergoing a tremendous shift in consciousness. Science and spirituality are meeting, and together they are conquering the new frontier: the mind.

We are starting to understand the power of our minds. Quantum physics, brain studies, new research on brain plasticity, breakthroughs in medical technology and imaging, as well as genetic engineering are producing a quantum shift and leap in consciousness. Spirituality, meditation, and affirmative visualization are transcending religion and blending with science. The new human for the twenty-first century is emerging.

I am fascinated by the speed of discoveries yet profoundly saddened by the pain we are experiencing. However, from my own life experience, I know that pain is my greatest teacher and the catalyst for my continuing transformation.

For some time, my intuition has been nudging me to write. The little voice within me kept on whispering, "Put down on paper your thirty years of clinical work in the field of addictions and family therapy."

My ego had many rationales and answers for why I should not carry through with that idea. "You are not a writer. You have nothing to say. Great minds have done it and done it much better. You don't have time. You're too old. You cannot polarize your energies into writing. You need to take care of serious business. Writing is not productive." Does any of this sound familiar?

Well, life usually gets our attention. Some recent movies and the latest research have validated my deep beliefs about forms of healing, transformation, and spirituality. This new validation gave my Authentic Self the necessary push, motivation, and passion to write about and further my lifetime work.

I have been on a spiritual quest all my life. My spiritual path has meant journeying down the road less traveled by doing my inner work for the past thirty-five years.

The pain of addictions led me to a healing process, but my soul's yearning attracted to me the teachers and teachings necessary to transform my life and to shape my life's mission.

I arrived on this planet on September 20, 1938 in Zagreb, the capital city of Croatia. Zagreb is one of the oldest cities in Europe and yet one of Europe's youngest metropolises. Its long history began with its founding in 1094, and in 1242, Zagreb was proclaimed a free royal city.

Zagreb was founded where the last hills of the Alps merge into the Pannonian Valley. The city is cradled between the Medvednica Mountain, its highest peak being Sljeme, and the Sava River. The city is at the crossroads of various cultures, religions, and nations.

In the seventeenth and eighteenth centuries, Zagreb was badly devastated by fire and the plague. The city was rebuilt during the Austro-Hungarian Empire's occupation with its architecture being inspired by Vienna. One of Zagreb's most recognizable landmarks is its neo-gothic cathedral. Begun in the late eleventh century, the cathedral was not fully completed until the nineteenth century. The cathedral's treasury contains priceless treasures and relics dating from throughout its long history. Zagreb is also marked with beautiful avenues lined with chestnut trees and gardens filled with lilacs and jasmine.

According to my parents, my arrival was a happy event. I was the firstborn and would be their only surviving child—my younger brother died two days after his birth and my sister was a stillbirth. For a long time, I was the only grandchild in the family. Then, when I was two years old, World War II erupted in Europe and the Germans soon occupied my country of origin.

Years later, a wise person told me that we choose the perfect environment for our spiritual growth; yes, the perfect environment to learn the lessons we need to learn so we can carry out our life's purpose. I have found that answer to be the logical explanation for why I grew up in the country I did and at that time in history.

My parents were sweet people, who had an important commonality point: their alcoholic fathers. Only when I started my own recovery did I truly understood the impact this simple truth had on their lives and on our family imprints.

You might wonder what are *imprints*: they are our emotional map, the deep-seated beliefs and values stored in our brain's limbic system. In spite of everything we know, our imprints govern our life at the subconscious level. Let me illustrate.

Have you ever been in a situation you found so painful and embarrassing that you told yourself, "I will never make this mistake again," only to see yourself a few days, weeks, or months later repeating the same mistake. The people and places may have been different, but the results were the same.

Did you ever, after ending a really bad relationship, swear you will never again get yourself into another such relationship, only to find that your next relationship is the same or worse than the previous one?

Have you said to yourself and perhaps to your friends that you will never be like your parents? You were sure you would never say the things they said, nor act the way they acted. Surprise! One day you hear yourself talking to your child and you sound, look, and act just like your parents—history has been repeated.

Your rational mind knows better; it knows what you do not want to be, to do, or to experience. So you wonder what is wrong with this picture. You ask yourself, "Why am I doing this?"

The answer is *imprint*. Our subconscious imprints are the deep-seated beliefs and messages we have received and internalized.

Once an imprint is internalized, it becomes a subconscious governing force in our lives. Our imprints form our emotional map, determining our ability to relate to self and to others. Imprints form our perceptions, values, and belief systems. Imprints determine the quality of our relationships with life, God, self, and others. Our values govern our choices as well as our behaviors. They determine whether we are reactive or pro-active.

The limbic system is the seat of our ability to connect with others and experience intimacy and love. It is also the seat of our imprints. Imprints form our emotional intelligence. Consequently, our imprints can enhance or sabotage our ability to connect, to form and sustain meaningful relationships with others.

Imprints can be broken down into two major categories: genetic and environmental. I will explore both in this book.

My purpose here is to take you on a journey of emotional, intellectual, social, cultural, and religious imprinting. In the first section of this book, I will illustrate for you the imprints I have developed during the past seventy-one years of my life;

then I will provide you with the information and tools I have learned about imprints and share stories of others who have been successful in overcoming their own negative imprints. By doing so, I hope you will be able to transform your own life, shed the imprints that hold you back, and find your Authentic Self. We will talk more about what is the Authentic Self in these pages as well.

I am very grateful for everything that has ever happened in my life. It does not matter if I have internalized it as good or bad. All of it was necessary to transform me into who I am today. It was the necessary path to my true Identity and Authentic Self. My story is the story of suffering transformed into lessons, gifts, and victories. More than that, it is the story of human spirit rising above circumstances, thereby allowing me to rewrite my history. My passion, my creativity, and my compassion for humanity were all born on that path.

My hope is that this book will be the catalyst of your own transformation and awakening to your Authentic Self. My greatest hope is that children of wars and children of oppression and abuse can find hope, dignity, and a path of transformation. My intent is to take you on a journey of rewriting your history, shifting your perceptions, and discovering the truth of your origin. Thank you for joining me along this path.

Part I:

My Personal Imprint Journey

1 Through the Eyes of a Child

In April 1941, I was two and a half years old. The Germans had just invaded my country and my hometown. Before World War II, Croatia was part of the Kingdom of Yugoslavia. It was technically a monarchy, ruled since 1934 by the young King Peter II, who would be forced to go into exile when the Axis powers invaded.

At that time, I was too young to understand what was happening, but I was aware of my parents' fear as they listened to the radio. An Independent State of Croatia had been formed—a clerical-fascist state. I didn't understand what any of that meant, but I felt my parents' fear and insecurity.

In the following months, my hometown no longer looked the same. Soldiers were everywhere. My parents did not take me to the park any longer. People whispered. Everything was strange. My mom still baked cookies, but she also cried a lot. I was still a child…now I was a scared little girl. *Why?*

The radio's volume was kept low. My dad was listening to the voice of America. My parents' faces had changed from smiles to worry. The laughter was gone. The blinds on the windows were always closed now; no longer was I allowed to play in the park. *Why?*

The answer was always the same, "Hush, baby; these are hard and dangerous times. You must be a good girl…don't make Mama cry."

I loved my mom; I didn't want to make her cry. I couldn't understand why nobody played or laughed anymore. Why was there no more music? Why couldn't we see the sky? Why were we in darkness? Why were the sirens screaming outside?

Early imprint: I internalized "Don't make Mama cry" to mean that other people's happiness is my responsibility. If they cry, it is my fault: I am not good enough.

My mother and father had a fashion salon in our home. Mom had a few ladies working for her and was always busy. My grandma, my mom's mom, was my primary babysitter.

Grandma was my storyteller. She told me tales about angels and spirits. While she gently brushed my blonde curly hair, Grandma told me how angels have beautiful blonde and silky hair. Listening to her sweet voice made me feel safe from the outside danger. Grandma said the angels were everywhere and would protect us from harm. I believed her. She said I had a beautiful and wise guardian angel who was always leading me on my path.

These stories created one of the positive Spiritual Imprints I have felt at work throughout my life: the feeling of being guided.

My favorite story from Grandma was about when she was a little girl and went to the family well to get some water. The cord was stuck around the wheel. Because she was too small to reach the cord, she climbed up onto the well wall to pull the cord. The cord got untangled, but the wheel started rolling and pulling my grandma into the well. Soon, she was hanging in the darkness and crying for help. That is when her guardian angel held her in her arms so she would not fall farther down into the well. Her angel sent for help by making Grandma's big brother worry about her. He went looking for her, heard her cry, and got her out. Grandma said we must always listen to the little voice within us as our angels always tell us what we must do. Grandma also had some scary stories about the devil and how bad and powerful he was. She was so scared of the devil that she could not even say his name. She called the devil the dishonorable one.

The religious imprint of my childhood was based on this duality of Good and Evil. It was based on external Power.

One of the ladies who worked for my mom was Melanka. She was my favorite of Mom's workers. She always came in with a smile. She loved pretty dresses and would talk to me about beautiful ladies in evening gowns going to the opera. I liked being with her, and I dreamed about the beautiful dresses I would wear when I grew up. Melanka had a way of shutting down my *Why? Why? Why?* She made dresses for my doll. Outside, it was scary, but when I was with Melanka and my dolls, I was still a little girl.

At Christmas in 1941, I was a little over three years old. That year, there was no smell of cookies, no suckling roasted pig, and no bread. Christmas Eve dinner was very quiet. My mom had made soup and a little cake. There were no toys. My Christmas present was a sweater my mom had made. My parents said that Saint Nick could not come because of the war. My mom cried because there were no toys for me. My dad said the war was destroying us. When I asked, "What is 'war'?" my dad said it was when Germans or bad people invaded other people's countries and killed people. My grandma said we needed to pray; she said it was the devil making the war happen.

At night in my bed, I asked my guardian angel to make the Germans go home and to protect us.

A few times a week, I would go to church with Grandma. We would go very early in the morning. The church smelled good. We lighted candles for all the dead people in our family and one big one for my grandfather. Grandma wanted Grandpa to stop drinking. She said the devil made him drink and he was a drunk. I thought Grandpa was great fun to be with even if he did smell funny. He sang songs to me, and he talked to me about big ships he sailed on when he was a merchant marine officer, and he told me about far away countries he had visited where there was peace. Grandma and I lighted a candle for peace. Grandma said God would make the Germans go home. I believed her.

One day, I asked my dad why his dad, my other grandpa, never came to visit. He said it was because my grandpa was a mean drunk and good for nothing. Dad told me not to ask any more questions about him.

Unconsciously, I internalized my parents' shame and embarrassment over their alcoholic fathers, and later down the line, this imprint would stay with me as my very own toxic shame.

One day after Christmas, Melanka came to work crying. When my mom asked her what was wrong, Melanka said that the Ustashi had taken her husband to a concentration camp. [In April 1941, separatist Croats from Ustasha, the fascist terrorist organization, set up in Zagreb an Independent Croat regime. The new state, organized on strictly fascist and authoritarian lines, collaborated in all atrocities with the Nazis. Ruthless cruelty and genocide were its trademarks.]

Through Melanka's sobbing, I heard her say, "He is innocent, but they will kill him." My mom tried to console and support her. I went to the corner to sit in my little chair and to cry. "Why are they going to kill us?" I wondered. Grandma said God would help us. I wished someone would tell me when. I knew then what fear was… it was when you couldn't breathe and you hoped no one would see you.

On Mardi Gras Day, my mom showed me the costume she used to wear to the Mardi Gras Ball. She was a princess. Mom said that when I grew up, I'd be able to wear her costumes and pearls to the ball and even her beautiful feathery masks. She had a mask that her father had brought her from Venice, Italy. I wondered whether she meant that by the time I was grown up, the Germans would be gone. I hoped soon there would be music and dancing again.

Zagreb in winter was a true winter wonderland. The trees were covered with snow and only the red cardinals stood out like little flowers. We lived in the suburb in a friendly neighborhood with big trees, beautiful gardens, and loving people. On Mardi Gras, the snow was gently falling and making our yard beautiful. My favorite cherry tree was heavily covered with snow; it looked peaceful. I was on the slope in our yard, on my sleigh and sliding down with my doll. I kept my doll warm in my sweater.

That morning, my dad had gone to the market hoping to get some meat and groceries because less and less food was available. As I was sliding down the hill, he came running back. Suddenly, I heard noise all around me. A lot of planes quickly filled the sky. My dad grabbed me and we ran inside. In the hurry of the moment, I lost my doll. She was lying out in the snow. I wanted to go outside to get her, but my dad said, "No. It is too dangerous."

Once we were inside, I heard my dad explaining that the convoy of Italian troops outside was delivering new ammunition to the local German headquarters, located in the high school at the end of our street. The entire football field, behind the school, had been turned into the Germans' ammunition depot. The air attack was by the Allies to stop the Germans from building up their ammunition depot. Of course, I didn't fully understand all of this.

Suddenly, explosions were going off all around us. All the windows in our home were blown to pieces. My mom pushed me under an arch separating the dining room from the living room.

My mom was on top of me. Her hand was grabbing my throat and her nails were going deep into my skin. I could not breathe. My dad was trying to cover both of us. He finally noticed that Mom, in her panic, was choking me, so he pulled her hands away. Mom and I were sobbing.

I was so scared. Why did Grandma say the Germans were going to go home? The shattering of china and glass, the deafening sounds of explosions, the piercing sounds of sirens would stay with me for years. These were the sounds of death and terror. Yet the sounds were nothing compared to the visual images that followed, revealed by the sudden silence.

Like in a horror movie, our home had been turned into a war zone. Pieces of trucks, tires, metal, and glass were covering our furniture. Walls were cracked; windows were blown out. The floors were covered with glass, pieces of china, and bricks. In the backyard, hanging on the tree branches were pieces of human bodies.

My dad heard someone crying in front of our house. He walked over the debris to a man lying on the street, dying. The pressure from the bombing had crushed every bone in the man's body. My dad and a neighbor tried to lift him up without success. The man died while my father was holding him. In silence, my dad returned inside our house and took me into his arms. We all sobbed together. I did not ask my parents why people kill. Instead, I said, "I hate the Germans." My mom told me I must never say that; nobody could ever hear me say that. On that day, my feelings were silenced.

Our friends came screaming to our house. They asked for our help. In their bedroom were the heads and arms of the Italian soldiers. The Italian truck full of soldiers had been blown to pieces. The street was covered in blood.

They said that my girlfriend's mom had suffered a nervous breakdown. I didn't know what that meant, but I thought she was also going to die. The entire neighborhood smelled of death and smoke because the fires kept burning all night around us. It reminded me of the devil and the Hell my grandmother had told me about.

That night, my parents listened to the BBC. The radio reporter said that the British precision pilots had carried out their mission. From that day on, my parents listened to the BBC in secret—no one must know.

Lying in bed that night, I realized that life would never be the same. I knew that the world was not safe. I knew that I hated mean people who killed. I didn't understand why people killed, but I did not ask. I didn't know why God did not send His angels. I decided something must be wrong with the stories my grandma had told me, but I did not know what.

After that first bombing, the city went dark every night, no lights, no power, so it could not be seen by planes above. At the end of our backyard was an unexploded bomb. No one came to remove it. No one dared to go near it.

I stopped sleeping in my own bed and went to sleep with my parents. I clung to my father. Fear was not just a feeling. Fear had become a permanent state of being that went hand in hand with a deep-seated sense that there was nothing any of us could do. That was my first experience with *powerlessness*. The innocence and safety of my infancy had been replaced with daily terror.

The imprint I internalized was: The world is unsafe. Do not trust. Others have power over my life. No one can save me—God did not show up. The power of violence wins. And the worst imprint: I am a victim.

Anyone who grew up during any war, anyone who grew up in an oppressive regime, anyone who grew up as an abused minority, anyone who grew up in a violent or abusive family, I know you are hearing me with your heart. You have been there with me. You know what sleepless nights are. You know what silenced feelings are. You know what fear does. You understand me. Children of war, children of oppression and abuse, my Soul hears your cries, and I know you understand my tears.

* * *

In the fall of 1942, I had just turned four. For my birthday, my mom gave me a new coat she had made from her old coat. She also made me a birthday card with a picture on it of a beautiful young lady wearing an evening gown. She told me that she loved me very much, and because she was a clothing designer, she said that when I grew up, she would make me beautiful dresses. I again wondered whether the war would be over and the Germans gone by the time I grew up.

One day that same fall, my dad and I were walking down the street on our way to the market. Across the street against the wall were twelve men and three German soldiers. The soldiers opened fire and the twelve men fell. The wall was covered in blood.

My dad picked me up, threw me over a fence, and jumped over himself. He held me on the ground until everything was silent and it was safe to move again. I thought about how when you die, there's a lot of blood running around.

In 1963 when I revisited Zagreb, I saw a commemorative engraving on that wall in memory of the twelve patriots who died while fighting to resist the German occupation.

The imprint I internalized was that Life and Death are violent.

During that same time period, the occupying forces imposed the following law: for every German or Ustashi soldier killed, three Croats would be killed or taken to a concentration camp. For every German or Ustashi officer killed, twenty-five Croats would be killed or taken to a concentration camp.

That fall of 1942, my mother and I rarely went to town. It had become too dangerous to go out of the house. My father was the one running errands and waiting in line for food. He had to go early in the morning to get in line. Food was becoming harder and harder to get. There was no more meat—it was rationed only to the German and Ustashi troops.

One early morning while my dad was out, a German officer was killed. As a result, my dad and some other men who just happened to be on the street were imprisoned and were going to be taken to the concentration camp in Germany. Somehow, my dad managed to send a message to my mom. In a panic, my mom and I went to the train station to see him.

All the men were in a cattle wagon and tied to the floor, waiting to be taken to the concentration camp. A feeling of powerlessness and terror overcame my mother and me. We only saw my dad for a minute before the soldiers pushed us away from the train. As the train's doors were closed, the last thing I saw were the tears on my father's cheeks.

I remember that day as a big turning point. I went numb. It was like I was not there and I was not feeling.

The imprint of Lack and Scarcity turned into a profound belief in Not Enoughness: There was not enough safety, not enough food, not enough money, not enough joy. And with my dad gone, there was no more HOPE.

Hard days and sleepless nights followed. As my grandmother brushed my hair, she told me to pray that God would hear my prayers and bring my daddy back. I wanted so badly to believe her. My mom cried every day. Only sadness and fear filled our home.

The imprint I learned was: Life is a Struggle, full of Pain and Suffering.

Three days after my dad's departure, Mom took me to Zagreb's beautiful cathedral. We were going to light candles for my dad's safe return.

It was a cloudy day. In front of the cathedral was a large plaza. On this day, the plaza was filled with German and Ustashi troops, and the bishop of my hometown was blessing them.

My last sense of hope and trust had been broken. Now I knew that something was really wrong with us. We were born on the wrong side of the street. God was for the Germans and they were going to kill my dad.

On that October day when I was four years old, God became a problem, not a solution. I knew we were alone and abandoned.

My grandmother's God of love and goodness had abandoned us. He was for the Fascists and against us. The fear of Hell was transformed into a conviction that we were in Hell. The voices of my Grandma's angels had been silenced.

All of you who have experienced abandonment know the loneliness that follows…and you hear me. You understand me. Years later, I understood that I was an old soul who chose to learn a lesson about forgiveness and compassion. But in 1942, my feelings were silenced. I must not make Mama cry. I must not say how I feel. I must be a good girl.

The Germans had a motto: "Deutschland über Alles", meaning "Germany above others." It meant that they were the superior race and we were inferior. The political party governing Croatia during the war endorsed that belief to justify genocides and ethnic cleansings...and the Church agreed.

People of the Balkans, Slavic people, were seen as a sub-culture to be dominated. They were seen as poor, uneducated, made for hard work, and people to be abused. Slavic women were seen as heavyset and made for hard labor.

Today, the rational mind of a seventy-two year old woman comprehends the falsehood of this statement. But as the scared little girl I was, I internalized these events differently.

For years, I have walked through life feeling inferior and ashamed of the primitiveness of the Balkans and my Slavic origins.

How my heart understands and resonates with the imprint of despair that slavery brings. How my heart embraces the lack of hope and dignity of those who were raised in apartheid. How strongly I hear the cries of those tortured, exploited, raped, and annihilated by dictatorial regimes. I understand your imprints and your powerlessness, as well as your fears that turn into hate. I also understand your confusion when all of this evil is done in the name of God.

How well and profoundly I know the falsehood of exclusive religions that pretend to possess the truth but kill in the name of God, that impose doctrines filled with hatred of others, but call themselves lovers of God. Religion of Fear to control the masses, I have experienced you firsthand.

Looking back, I now know when and where my deep-seated feelings and imprints of unworthiness, inferiority, and disempowerment started—in a cultural, social, and religious imprint, the kind that permeates every aspect of one's life.

* * *

Life without my father was hard. It was the period of sleepless nights as well as nights filled with nightmares. My mom tried to reassure me the best she could, but I also felt responsible for her worries, helplessness, and despair.

Without us knowing and being aware of it, codependency had already become our way of relating to each other. We felt responsible for other people's feelings and ignored or silenced our own.

A clear imprint came from that period: Security comes only through a man, my dad. Women must have a man to protect them...but he was not there, so we were abandoned; therefore, men are unavailable.

For months, we did not know where my dad was or whether he was alive. A client of my mom, who was her classmate in college, was married to an officer. Through her intervention, my mom managed to find out that my dad was in

Buchenwald Concentration camp. We could not communicate with him, but we were relieved that he was still alive.

I did not know whether my Guardian angel still existed, but that night, I asked her to protect my dad and to bring him back. There was no reassurance, no whisper or sign, yet I did sleep that night.

The winter of 1942-43 was harsh and the world around us was filled with hatred and fear, hunger and greed. Survival was the main focus. My mom's uncle was a baker. He looked after my mom and me the best he could. He would bring us wood and coal for heat when he could. Sometimes, he would bring some bread and some bones for soup. Each time he came he looked more tired, old, and frail. My mom would talk in a very low voice to him. Everything became a silent secret. Survival meant being silent.

Many nights, the American planes would drop "carpet bombs," which were a series of bombs attached together. When they were released, they would light up so that the city lit up like it was daylight. The carpet bombs were used to destroy military targets, but parts of the city would be destroyed too.

We lived in a duplex. We were in the lower apartment and the top apartment was rented to our friends—that was where my girlfriend and her brother lived. Every night when the sirens went off, our friends would come running down to our apartment because it was safer. My mom would then hide us children in a closet to keep us safe. It was so dark in there. We were so scared, and my girlfriend would always get sick, but after a while, we started playing a game and guessing where the bombs would fall.

When reality is too painful, detach and medicate. Turn the pain into a game.

Needless to say, for years after that, I had an aversion for small dark spaces. I also had the ability to be deluded about reality or to deny it. *If I don't see it…it is not there. Even the war can become the White Elephant in the living room that no one can see.*

Looking back, I admire the resilience and courage of my people who fought back and survived. I have realized the richness of my people: the beauty, warmth, and passion of the Slavic people. I remember the courage of our survival under the hardest circumstances. I remember our creativity and resourcefulness. I remember the goodness of our hearts. Most importantly, I realize that my earlier rejection of my people was also my rejection of myself.

The big imprint from that period of my history: I have no right to exist.

At the same time, by stopping my identification with a country or culture—not through rejection or denial but by realizing I don't have to be limited by that identification, my Authentic Self has come to life. By not identifying with a nation, country, or culture, I accept that my true origin is Divine. It is only when I have truly embraced and aligned myself with God, as I understand God, that I become One with all. I truly feel the blessing of multiple citizenships. I truly feel the privilege of speaking three languages. Three windows to different cultures:

Croatian, French, and English. What a blessing. It allows me to be One with all. My Spirit is truly free of borders, language, barriers, religious dogmas…and that allows me to be an observer. To come to this Realization, I did have to take the road less traveled.

Beyond knowing that my dad was alive, we had no news of him. Fear was our permanent state of being. Surviving another day was considered a success.

My grandma was still praying, still giving money to the Church and lighting candles for my dad's return, for peace, and for Grandpa to quit drinking. My mom was getting angrier with her mother and her obsession with the Church. My mom was also angry at her father because he embarrassed her with his drinking.

Mom's fear turned into anger and trying to control everything. She was angry at the war and its atrocities. She was angry at the family war caused by alcoholism and Grandma's religious addiction. She always seemed in those days to be screaming, crying, or just staying busy—perhaps so she did not have to think and worry.

No one had time for me. By the summer of 1943 when I was four and a half years old, I was already an old person in a child's body.

One day, Melanka read to us a letter received from her husband who was in a concentration camp run by Ustashi. He described the tortures he and the other prisoners there were enduring. His friend had just died after the Ustashi pulled out his hair and nails. Hearing this horror story, my mom got sick and could no longer listen.

As I listened to the details, unknowingly, I formed an important imprint: Power/Authorities are mean and violent. Do not trust Authorities.

Melanka's husband asked for our prayers, but in my mind I knew prayer would not work. God was for the Germans—I knew because I had seen the bishop blessing them.

War, religion, abuse, and death were becoming synonymous in my imprints. To this day, I do not watch violent movies about torture and killings. They go against every fiber in me. They violate my humanity as well as all humanity.

The year of 1943 was the period of hopelessness, helplessness, and loneliness. We all felt stuck without a light at the end of the tunnel.

I am so grateful that my spiritual beliefs have healed and transformed my life. Radical forgiveness has transformed fear and hatred into love, compassion, and understanding.

In the summer of 1943, the Germans were having serious problems on the Russian front. They were using prisoners from concentration camps as human shields to protect the German army.

Unknown to my family, my dad was among those prisoners. However, before the Battle of Kursk in July 1943, my dad managed to escape with another prisoner. They fled into the woods, and at night, they tied themselves under a train going to Ukraine and Romania. During the daytime, they hid in the woods, and sometimes, a Russian peasant hid them and gave them some food. It took them from July until the beginning of November to reach Zagreb.

When my dad reached home, he was physically ill. The malnutrition, hard labor, beatings, humidity, and cold of the concentration camp and the Russian front had taken their toll. He was physically burnt out, but he was alive. What a relief I felt to see him! He was emotionally broken also, but I did not understand that then. I only knew he was alive and I hoped that meant things would be more normal again.

I did not understand then that in the concentration camp, my dad had been forced to witness death on a daily basis. When he returned home, he did not know how to deal with such loss, grief, and death, so he stayed silent about it. His very presence in our home also required silence. We kept it a secret from most people and he rarely went outside.

The Germans were experiencing more and more difficulties as the Allies continued to advance from all sides. In frustration and fear, the Ustashi in Croatia and the Chetniks in Serbia and Montenegro were multiplying the killings and atrocities they committed.

However, Tito and the Partisans—the Yugoslav Resistance—were gaining in the mountains of Bosnia. Tito was a Communist leader and the Resistance was turning Communist too.

By the spring of 1945, the German army and its puppet governments were in full retreat before the Yugoslav Partisans. On May 14 and 15, 1945 the Battle of Poljana was fought between Ustashi and Partisan troops. Although the Germans had surrendered on May 7th, in Yugoslavia the war ended with that battle.

Zagreb experienced its last battle in the form of street fights. For two days, we were barricaded in our home as the fighting continued all around our house. As the Ustashi retreated, they dynamited sections of the town to prevent the Partisans from advancing.

During this time, we were very hopeful that the American troops would liberate Croatia. But that did not happen. Although the British were involved in Poljana, Croatia was "liberated" by the arrival of Partisans, followed by the Russian troops.

The Partisans took over the city. Soon the streets were lined with sick, wounded, battered, and hungry soldiers, some of whom were hardly more than sixteen years old and some were old men. They brought with them their sick horses. The smell in the streets was horrific.

While we were all happy and relieved that the Germans and Ustashi were gone, we were also afraid; no one knew what these Communist troops would do. What was the future going to be like?

2 A Post-War Life: History Repeated

In September 1945, I was seven years old. The Russian army had replaced the Germans, and our friends were forced to take in a Russian General with his chauffeur.

After the initial relief at the end of the war, day-by-day fear began to return. Tito's Communist regime was doing a cleansing. The witch-hunt for Nazi collaborators was on. Once again people were being imprisoned or executed. Yet the new government was promising a better day.

Such a big part of the country had been damaged and destroyed by the war. The housing crisis was at an all time high. A food and clothing shortage continued. Factories had been destroyed. A five-year reconstruction plan was put into effect, and everyone was forced to "volunteer," even the children.

We were all going to be equal. That meant that the little left of our lives was to be taken away. The Communists nationalized everything. Our duplex was nationalized. Next, it was our three-bedroom apartment. My parents received a notice that some strangers were going to occupy two rooms while we lived in one room and shared the kitchen and our bathroom with these people.

Private enterprise was no longer allowed. My mom had to close her salon. My dad had been a tailor by profession, but now he had to go work at the army's factory. My mom was ordered to produce army coats.

New authorities; same abuse. New authorities once again had power over our lives and simply perpetuated the feeling of powerlessness. The Victim Imprint was faithfully being played out.

In the fall of 1945, I started school. It was supposed to be a happy time in my life. Instead, it turned out to be a time of conflict. My teachers said that God did not exist. In the Communist doctrine, there is no God. I had already come to that belief because of the war, or at least, that if there were a God, He had abandoned us.

My mom was stuck between her belief in democracy and freedom of choice and her family's pressure to raise me as a Catholic. My mom's middle sister was a nun.

In spite of my mom's struggles with religion, and my own struggles, my mom finally insisted that I would make my first communion.

I did not feel safe inside the church. The only thing I liked about it was the smell and the candles, and making my first communion had one bonus—the beautiful white dress my mom made for me. But my trust in God had been broken. I could not believe in Him any longer.

My imprint that God was against us and had abandoned us was now being challenged by the Communist theory that God did not exist. My best solution was to deny my inner conflict and that of the people around me...to pretend it wasn't there.

The consequence of my mom's decision that I make my first communion was that I was to be thrown out of school and my family would be put on the black list. But because my mom was an activist and a fighter for civil rights, she managed to keep me in school. Because she turned her fear into anger, she found the courage to fight.

My mother had been a college professor who had hardly had a chance to teach. After she had graduated, she had taught for a short time, but then she had gotten married and had me. When she was ready to go back to teaching, the war had broken out and opportunities for women were not there.

After the war, my mother's need for justice, women's rights, and freedom of religion got her in trouble with the authorities, who would not tolerate resistance. She was often on their black list, which meant no food stamps, and no sugar or coffee for the month. She even had a restraining order against her, denying her the right to leave the city without permission.

Early in her life, as the oldest of three daughters, my mother had taken on the role of hero and caretaker in her family. Today, I understand how her self-image and self-worth were deeply imprinted with shame over her father's alcoholism and public drunkenness. The shame was coupled with her feelings of inadequacy because she was not able to save him from his alcoholism.

My grandmother's religious devotion, which today would be understood as an addiction to religion because it was so extreme, only made matters more difficult for my mother. The entire family was in denial about my grandfather's alcoholism, and my grandmother used religion to cope with it. At that time, alcoholism was not understood as a disease but viewed as a moral issue. My grandma believed that if she gave the church more money, if she lit more candles, then she could drive the devil out of my grandpa. My aunt the nun was convinced that a few more novenas and rosaries would do the same thing.

My mom and her parents used to argue to no avail about religion and my grandpa's drinking. My grandpa kept drinking, and my mom kept resenting. With her low self-image, my mother attracted into her life a man with a similar background—my father was also the son of an alcoholic, and on top of that, my paternal grandfather was a sex addict and a gambler. In those days, people didn't understand about sex addiction so he would have simply been referred to as a womanizer.

My dad was raised in an environment of fear, shame, and poverty that made him grow up feeling inadequate. His father left Croatia for the United States when he was just a little boy. When he was fifteen, my dad went to join his father in New York, during the time of alcohol prohibition in the United States. My paternal grandfather was then living in a house of prostitution that was also a speak-easy and gambling joint. His addictions were in full swing. When my father saw what his father had become, he swore he would never do the same, but some imprints are genetic.

My two sweet parents were the adult children of alcoholics, who never got any help. These two brave souls, with courage, resilience, and great work ethics, tried to build a post-war life. They were constantly busy just trying to survive—my mom had little time for me, and my father was constantly worried about losing what little we had.

My parents were imprinted with Scarcity and a sense of Not Enoughness: Not enough security, not enough time, not enough money. The Not Enough Syndrome permeated all aspects of our lives. We were not enough, we did not have enough, and we never did enough to fix it. Unfortunately, the less my parents had, the more they tried to Control. Added to this imprint was the belief that all of our good comes from outside. Someone else had the power to withhold what we should have viewed as rightfully ours, so we were Helpless and unable to improve the situation.

Addictions are a serious disease, but they are treatable. However, because back then they were viewed as a moral issue, a personal shortcoming with social and religious stigma attached, people tried to deny, hide, and minimize the addictions to save themselves and their families from shame. Still today, denial and minimization are the greatest obstacles to overcome in order to recover from the effects of addictions upon a family. Because addictions are a family disease, they corrode the bonds of trust between family members, destroying relationships and individuals. Today help is available to overcome these situations, as I'll address later in this book, but unfortunately, my grandfathers and my family did not get the necessary help.

From 1945 to 1949 in post-war Croatia, it was easy to believe there was not enough of anything. All of post-war Croatia and post-war Europe was struggling.

President Tito made a valiant effort to hold together six Republics: Croatia, Serbia, Slovenia, Montenegro, Macedonia, and Bosnia/Herzegovina. This diversity represented four languages and three religions: Catholic, Orthodox, and Muslim. Under his rule, Tito managed to contain the mistrust, anger, and mutual hatred among this mixture. Tito had the courage to stand up to the Russians and get them out of the country. He turned Yugoslavia into a Socialist state rather than a Communist one, and by managing to forge alliances with the Western nations, he preserved a type of autonomy for Yugoslavia. Within this shaky political environment, I was growing up.

3 A Turning Point

On Palm Sunday 1949, I was ten and a half years old. It was a beautiful sunny day and the first spring flowers were blooming. My mom took me to church. I liked going with her; it was our special time together.

On the way to church, Mom would talk to me about Jesus. She said that he was her friend and that Jesus taught her how to love and forgive. She said that we must forgive all those who have hurt us. I asked her whether that meant we needed to forgive all the people who had killed others during the war. In her soft voice, she replied, "Yes, especially them, and that's hard, which is why we need Jesus' help."

While attending Mass, I kept thinking about those words. Because the Mass was in Latin, I could not understand it so I was bored. When I looked at my mom, I saw tears on her cheeks. I wondered whether Mom knew I was bored, and it made her cry that I did not pay attention, but when I took her hand, she gently pulled me toward her and whispered in my ear, "My belly hurts and I am in pain."

When the Mass was over, instead of walking home like we intended, we took the tramway. While we were on the tram, Mom collapsed and fainted. People gathered around and helped her. She regained consciousness while I was crying. I asked her friend Jesus to help her get better.

When we reached home, Mom took my face in her hands and held it tenderly. She told me that she loved me a lot. Then she explained that she had been sick for a while and that she needed to go to the hospital. She said that no matter what happened she would always be with me and love me.

That was the last time I saw my mom walking. She went to the Zagreb Gynecological Hospital, the same one where I was born, and where my brother and sister had been born and had died. I wondered whether Mom's illness meant that she was going to have another baby who would die. I knew how much my dad wanted a son—none of his brothers had sons so if he did not have one, our family name would end.

But when I asked Mom whether she was going to have a baby or if she had lost a baby like last time, she said, "No, I have leukemia." Then Dad told me that Mom was tired, so I mustn't ask her any more questions. Somehow, I knew Mom's illness was like the radio during the war—a secret we could not talk about.

The spring and summer of 1949 was a sad time. Mom was home in bed, most of the time in pain or sleeping. Dad was constantly crying, and he rarely let me see Mom because he didn't want me to disturb her rest. I held my dolls and told them stories about how my mom would make beautiful dresses for all of us when we grew up. Because the house was so quiet, I sang to my dolls the nursery rhymes Mom used to sing to me.

My dad did not know emotionally how to handle grief and loss. He could not bear the thought that my mother was dying. He also felt he needed to protect me from death and loss, so he decided to send me to summer camp so I would not be there when Mom passed away.

I was on the Adriatic Sea at a children's camp on August 14, 1949 when my mom made her transition into the other world. The night before, she came to me in a dream. She looked beautiful. She said she must go because her pain was too great, but she would not be far and her spirit would always be with me. She gave me her blessing, and she asked me to be a good and brave girl; she told me she would see me again.

When I woke up on August 14th, I knew my mom was gone. Despite what my mom had told me in my dream, as a little girl I had a hard time not losing sight of her message. Her death was the greatest loss in my life to date.

As I am writing this passage, I just realized I am writing on August 14, 2009, exactly sixty years later. Thank you, Mom, for showing up on the anniversary of your death. I salute and celebrate your life, a short life—you were thirty-six years old when you left—but a life of great impact.

The imprint I internalized regarding my mom's death was: Love does not last...it will abandon you. I am not good enough to be loved. That imprint would play a large role in my relationships.

My dad's war traumas prevented him from dealing with my mother's loss. When I returned home, he could not tell me the truth. It took two days and my confronting him before he could tell me that Mom had passed away, that her funeral was over, and that now it was just him and me. At the time, I did not understand about the trauma my father had gone through during the war that made him unable to cope with my mother's loss. All I knew was that I felt like he did not want me there.

From that day on, my father went into a deep depression. To help him cope, I became the caretaker of his feelings. Intuitively, I sensed that I had become the parent while he became the child. I felt that taking care of him was what was expected of me. For a whole year, I was the cook who made sure Dad had his breakfast. I was "a good girl" like Mom had told me to be. The house was clean, but my heart felt empty because my father was no longer emotionally there for me, and I would cry myself to sleep at night.

Unconsciously, this experience produced a huge imprint on me that would affect me in the future: You cannot trust a man; you cannot count on a man...men don't show up! I am alone. I must have control in order to survive.

The lack of closure with my mother because I was not with her when she died was a huge resentment I carried with me for years. Because my father had prevented me from being with her at the end, and because he was the only one I could place blame on, I resented and blamed him for my mother's illness and death.

Now that the war was over and my mom was gone, my dad was so fed up with Europe that he wanted to go back to the United States. He had lived there with his father before the war and had only come back to Croatia to visit his mother and sisters, but while visiting, he had met my mom and gotten married, and then I was born not long before the war began. Now he felt it was best to return to the United States.

My dad also wanted a "new mother" for me, someone who would take care of me. So he started dating a seamstress who worked with him at the army factory. One day he brought her home to meet me, and she gave me a blouse she had made and also some dresses for my doll. When dad said this woman would be my new mom, I thought to myself, "That is not going to happen."

Nevertheless, in December 1949, my dad married my step-mom. She was a good, hardworking woman. But, she was also the second child of an alcoholic father who had been physically and emotionally abusive to her, causing her to be rebellious. As a result, her imprints and self-image were similar to those of my father. Because I had just lost my mom, I had a hard time embracing her. Even though she was nice to me, we had a rough beginning.

My imprints from first having a stepmother: Don't Trust, and Love does not last. I felt if Love lasted, my father would not forget my mother by marrying my stepmother. These feelings stood in the way of my relationship with her. Her imprint was: Nobody loves me so I won't love anyone else. We ended up competing for my father's attention.

In 1949, Croatia was a Communist country with strictly closed borders. No one was allowed to travel to the West without a really good reason. Then in the early spring of 1950, my father's brother, who lived in Paris, suddenly died of food poisoning. My father took advantage of this situation to apply for passports. He told the officials that we needed to attend the funeral and resolve the estate, and then we would return to Zagreb.

We got the passports, packed three small suitcases, and left. No one in the extended family knew we were leaving or that we had left without any intention to return. We kept the rest of the family in the dark as a precautionary measure in case later they would be interrogated by the secret police. My dad was determined to get us to the United States as soon as possible.

Over the course of sixteen months, my life had changed completely: I had lost my mom, my country, my language, my school, my friends, and my toys. I had lost the comfort of my maternal grandmother's presence and her stories; I had lost the rock of faith that she was in my life. Worst of all, I had lost a part of myself. I was hurt, grieving, and confused.

But long before that time, I had already learned what to do with my feelings: silence and repress them; hold my breath, go numb, and be busy so I didn't have to think. I did not understand then that when I held my breath and went numb, my nervous system only anchored the negative perception, sending the imprint deeper into my subconscious mind to turn it into a belief—a belief that would only do me harm later in my life.

4   The New and the Old

At twelve years of age, traveling to Paris on the Orient Express was an adventure. Movies had been made about the Orient Express, and it traveled through famous places: from Istanbul to Paris. It was beautiful, and I was very impressed by it and the entire journey. It was my first long trip to a foreign country, and I was going to see the great places I had only heard about in my maternal grandfather's stories. It was an exciting trip full of new places to discover.

But the journey was a bit frightening when we began. At the Yugoslav/Italian border, the soldiers searched everything and everyone. My step-mom and I were taken away from my father and placed in a wagon with only women and children where we were told we had to undress. Terror came running back to me. My first thought was "They are going to take my father away from me," and my mind kept replaying my memory from the war of him in a cattle train going to Germany.

When the soldiers were finished searching us, we were sent back to join my dad. We then were allowed back on the train and from the border went to Venice. We were not allowed to get off the train in Venice because we only had a French visa. Vendors were selling sandwiches and candy, but we could not understand what they were saying in Italian. I wanted some candy, but my father said it cost too much.

A French gentleman on the train saw me looking at the candies. He motioned to the vendor to give him a bag of chocolate candy and a sandwich. He handed me both and said something in French, but I could not understand him. I took the sandwich and candy and said, "Thank you," in Croatian.

As I was eating, I was swallowing my tears. I had just realized I could not understand people who spoke to me in strange languages. What would I do in Paris? How would I talk to people? That was the first time it registered with me that I had just lost all that was familiar.

A new imprint became stamped upon me: I am different and ignorant. My previous imprint—as a Slavic female I am inferior—was reinforced. Little did I know how those imprints would manifest themselves in my future.

We arrived in Paris early in the morning. My dad spoke in English and German to a conductor to ask for directions to the address where my uncle's widow lived. They had a hard time understanding each other, but after awhile, we understood to go on a train heading for the suburb of Asnieres.

From the train's window, I first saw Paris. Wow! Never, not even in pictures, had I seen a more beautiful city. It made Zagreb look so small. People were nicely dressed and smiling. No soldiers were on the streets. Everything looked so bright.

Finally, we arrived at *3 Rue de Strasbourg* with our little suitcases. Aunt Suzanne's apartment was on the third floor of a large apartment complex. Aunt Suzanne was a petite woman with beautiful blue eyes. She greeted us with hugs, but we could not understand what she said to us. When she realized we could not speak French, she went to get her neighbor Mademoiselle Shoerer who spoke German.

My dad explained to Mademoiselle Shoerer that we needed a place to stay for a very short time because we were going to the United States. He also said we needed a shoemaker to remove his shoe's heal because he had hidden forty American dollars there—that was our fortune.

Mademoiselle Shoerer and Aunt Suzanne had a long conversation that sounded very serious. Finally, Mademoiselle Shoerer told my father that Aunt Suzanne would give us her apartment while she would move in with her sister.

Mademoiselle Shoerer took my dad to the shoemaker and then to get some groceries while my step-mom and I helped Aunt Suzanne to pack. We also unpacked our own little suitcases.

Mademoiselle Shoerer turned out to be the guardian angel my grandma used to talk about. Although the Germans had killed her two brothers, and her fiancé had died fighting in the French Resistance, she still had a heart of gold. Besides helping us to communicate and teaching us where to go in Paris, she gave us a folding bed for me to sleep on.

Aunt Suzanne's apartment was a small place consisting of one bedroom, one toilet, and one kitchenette 6' x 4'. It had no shower or bath, but we were grateful. My dad kept reminding us, "Now we are free and soon we will be in the U.S."

But two days later, when my dad went to the U.S. Embassy to apply for our visas, he learned that the U.S. Government's immigration quota was full so no more visas were being issued, and there was an eight-year waiting period. That meant we would have to live in Paris for eight years. My father applied for the visas anyway, hoping for a miracle. He also decided to apply for a visa at the Canadian Embassy—Canada's waiting list was only six years by comparison.

Thus began an incredible chapter in our lives. We could not move to the United States or Canada as my father had originally planned, and we could not go back to Croatia since it was part of Communist Yugoslavia with closed borders. My parents' need for freedom and my father's hope for a better life in "America" kept us going.

Our French visas were valid only for six months, not six years. In 1950, French laws for immigrants had specific requirements—we could not remain in France without a working permit, and we could not get a working permit without a residency permit. The situation was a classic catch-22 and confirmed more deeply our family imprint of victimhood.

After numerous pleas, we became "DP" meaning Displaced Persons. No status, no belongings, no rights. Five times we were scheduled for deportation back to Croatia. Had we gone back there, my father would have been thrown in prison for leaving the country without intent to return. Somehow through Divine Intervention, we managed to stay in France. My dad's determination, courage, resilience, resourcefulness, and strong survival skills always found the right connections to prolong our stay. Throughout this time, Aunt Suzanne was an Angel of Grace, who kept living with her sister so we could use her little apartment.

In the autumn of 1950, I was twelve years old, but I could not be enrolled in a regular school because I did not speak French. Instead, I started attending classes at l'Alliance Francaise, a school for foreign students and displaced persons who were in need of learning the French language.

I worked very hard at studying the French language so I would be able to go to a regular school and not lose too much time, although I expected one school year would be lost. Still, I emulated my parents' survival skills and strengths. We had resilience, resourcefulness, hope, and courage. Looking back, I am amazed at the courage we developed during this time of so much adversity and pain. Besides the regular curriculum offered at the l'Alliance Francaise was a crash course in French; taking it quickly paid off—I was allowed to take the exam and passed. I was enrolled in the public school halfway into the school year. My workaholic tendencies had started to be developed out of necessity.

Once I started attending the public school, I found I was an outcast. My French had a strong Slavic accent. I wore my step-mom's hand-me-down clothes and dressed according to my father's strict code of modesty. My clothes were too big, too old, and too conservative. In a city of fashion, I really stood out. I was different. I did not blend in. I did not belong. I was a displaced person.

Children can be cruel. I was called *maudit polack*, meaning "damn Polack." They laughed at my clothes, my accent, and at me. My self-image, my self-worth, and my body-image were shattered. My imprints and deep-seated beliefs were now being validated: *I am not good enough, not pretty enough, and not smart enough. I am not lovable.* My imprints were now manifesting into reality as proven by how my fellow students were treating me.

How my heart goes out to all children of immigrants wherever they are. Sweet, hardworking, bright souls who are ridiculed, rejected, and humiliated. How I understand with a heart full of compassion my own parents and their struggle with their own self-images and self-worth. These were not times for child psychology; these were times of bare survival.

Due to the language barrier and their own lack of education, my dad and step-mom could not help me with my schoolwork; nor could they afford a tutor for me. I felt lost and overwhelmed. Mostly, I felt lonely and different.

My loneliness had to do with my imprints: *I cannot trust anyone; there is no one to help. The Catholic God of my childhood was for the Germans and against us. I am alone and separate from All.* This last imprint would follow me through all my relationships.

However, a Divine Imprint that stayed with me was my maternal grandmother's stories of good spirits and angels. My mother coming to me in my dream just before she died had reinforced for me that my grandmother's stories were true; furthermore, my mother had told me she would always be with me.

Intuitively, I started talking to my mom's spirit and to my guardian angel, asking them for help, asking them for solutions to my scholastic problems. I did not realize at the time that I was developing a strong inner life and an intuitive connection to something higher. I started to be guided, inspired, and shown in my dreams the solutions to mathematical problems I did not understand. I still studied hard, but I came to rely more and more on my inner guidance.

Often, my mom would come in my dreams to help me with my schoolwork. In those dreams, I would clearly see what I needed to do; I was able to memorize the answers shown in my dreams and pass exams successfully. Without knowing it, my inner wisdom and my survival skills were being developed.

Nevertheless, my inner conflicts continued. Trusting my dreams and intuition worked well with my schoolwork, but my self-image and self-worth were still influenced and directed by my negative imprints, which would affect all my relationships.

5   The Vista of Possibilities

At twelve years old, I was impressionable and truly impressed by Paris. Paris, that beautiful city of light, art, architecture, culture, and refinement, was fascinating in my eyes. Paris the capital of fashion, gorgeous women, and romance, made me dream. Even post-war Paris was a vibrant metropolis of abundance, prosperity, opulence, and beauty.

In Croatia, I had not known that we were poor—everyone was. In Paris, my realization of our poverty reinforced my imprint of scarcity and developed my driving force to succeed. *The imprints of "I am what I do" and "I am what I have"* were defining me. Imprints are truly the emotional map dictating experiences and behaviors. At that age, I did not know the Greater Truth about my being; nor did I know about my Authentic Self.

What comes with the belief of "not enough" is the feeling of never being satisfied. I felt the sensation of craving and waiting for something better to come along, and by extension, I developed unrealistic expectations of myself, of others, and of life.

Not to have, do, or be enough means to be constantly living in the future. It is waiting for something or someone to give you a sense of security. It is the belief that our happiness and security must and will come from something or someone external to us. However, for some people, the opposite is true—the belief in "not enough" will keep them living in the past, recounting the losses, lacks, and hurts. In either case, one is unable to be in the "Now" moment appreciating what is.

At twelve, I was not living in the past; I was living in the future. The French shaped my love of culture, languages, and art. They gave me my appreciation for fashion, elegance, and aesthetic beauty. I fell in love with the city, and I wanted so badly to belong there, so I started to assimilate into French culture despite my parents maintaining their comfort zone of living in the Croatian ghetto of Paris. While my speaking the language opened doors for me, not knowing French kept my parents isolated.

Four years went by while we lived in Paris and I assimilated to French ways, including fashion. When we celebrated my "sweet sixteen" birthday, my father gave me my very first pair of nylons and my first pair of fashionable shoes. My step-mother made me some new clothes. Because my stepmother was a gifted seamstress, Christian Dior had hired her in its new Ready-to-Wear department. Whenever the suits or dresses my stepmother made were in Dior's window on the Champs Elysées, we would go to admire them. Not far from there was the famous Hotel George V. Ladies in beautiful evening gowns were stepping out of limousines and going for dinner at its Le Cinq Restaurant. I remember standing in awe of them, and I made a firm decision that some day I would be there, dressed in my finest with my Prince Charming. Life definitely started to have a sense of normalcy and possibilities.

I was working very hard in school. I mastered French and was allowed to take exams to finish two school years in one. I completed the lycée (high school) and enrolled in art school. Life seemed full of promises.

We were still living in Aunt Suzanne's one room apartment. That room became my parents' working/sewing room. To pay for my art school, I helped them with the sewing, and I also knitted sweaters and other items for neighbors and acquaintances.

Thursday afternoons were a special treat for me because my class would go to the Louvre Museum and our teacher would give us a history lesson about the great artists that helped us to understand and appreciate their art. My teacher's lessons impacted my passion for color and form, and they gave me an unending love and appreciation for Michelangelo's genius. My sensitivity and talents were being nurtured and developed.

On Friday nights, my stepmother and I would go to movies. The films were always preceded by a live performance, so we got to see many famous singers at the beginning of their careers and such already famous performers as Edith Piaf and Charles Trenet. We even went to the Opera once in awhile. I was the official translator for my stepmother so she could understand the songs and storylines.

I was starting to feel a part of French life. I finally had made some good friends, and I even fell in love with a romantic French boy in my class who wrote me poems and gave me my first French kiss. I started to have a sense of stability, peace, and happiness.

Then the news came from the Canadian embassy. We had to appear for a hearing because the embassy was ready to issue our immigrant visas for Canada.

My old imprints of "What you love leaves you; you do not deserve love" were right back at work. Imprints make you either sabotage yourself or reproduce events that will confirm the basic belief.

My stepmother and I did not want to leave Paris; however, my father was determined to return to North America. He no longer believed a good life was possible in Europe. He wanted to have the American Dream.

When the time came to depart, my boyfriend and I cried and promised each other to write every day. Once again, with a broken heart, I left all that was familiar, beautiful, and safe.

6 The American Dream

The people at the Canadian Embassy told us that the best place for us in Canada would be Montreal in the Province of Quebec. It sounded like the most logical place to go since the French Canadians spoke French. So we made the decision to immigrate to Montreal.

In August 1955, we embarked on a Conrad Line transatlantic ship in *Le Havre* and off we went to "America."

I was seventeen years old and grieving for Paris, my boyfriend, and my art school. I certainly did not share my father's enthusiasm for America. I got seasick and spent seven nights sleeping in a lounge chair on the deck of the ship. The sea was rough and I could not eat. Similarly, my step-mom was grieving Christian Dior. My dad kept trying to convince us of the rightness of his decision, but he could not pull us out of our grief and we both ended up blaming him for "dragging" us to Canada.

It did not take very long after we arrived to discover that although Quebec was a French-speaking province, it was on an English-speaking continent, so in order to succeed, you had to speak English.

In 1955, Montreal looked like a small provincial town compared to Paris. The Law of Attraction was definitely at work in our lives—because we focused on lack, that's what we saw around us. French Canada was white, Catholic, and ruled by the English. Its people gave off an impression of being oppressed, inferior, and inadequate—feelings we knew so well from being immigrants and Slavic. Still, emotionally I felt at ease with the French Canadians. I even had a sense of French arrogance and superiority because I had just come from Paris.

The hidden gift of my imprints and growing up with a sense of lack meant I had truly developed some incredible life strengths and skills. I am humbled and amazed at the creativity of the human mind and its ability to make you adapt so you can survive. Through all my geographical moves, I have developed adaptability skills, resourcefulness, resilience, and an intuitive sense of orientation. You can put me in any city and any circumstance and I will find my way. Like the song says, "I'll survive." Determined, I learned to speak English.

Gone was my dream of art school. My father could not afford it. His first job in Montreal was as a dishwasher in a restaurant in Chinatown. My stepmother also became a dishwasher but at a restaurant in a department store—far gone for her were the days of Christian Dior on the Champs Elysées. But we remained grateful for what we had. Unlike in France, we were now legal immigrants, not displaced persons. We also now had our own two-bedroom apartment in my dad's name. We no longer had to fear being deported to Croatia, we had food, and we were healthy.

I started to attend a public business college to learn bookkeeping and secretarial skills so I could get a 9-5 job in an office. Once again, hope and resilience came to my rescue. During those early years we lived in Montreal, we watched the city continue to grow. By 1967, Montreal was a vibrant cosmopolitan city, a true crossroads of nations, and it became our home in a land of possibilities.

Due to their lack of education and failure to learn French or English, my parents slowly formed their Croatian ghetto with others like them. It became their comfort zone that protected them from their inadequacies, fears, and sense of inferiority. I was expected to be part of that community, but I could not.

Languages open new doors and vistas. They give us access to different cultures and points of view. I could not be boxed in. My imprint of shame over my origins made me reject the Croatian ghetto, and instead, I let the French culture shape and mold my values. Many times I felt split between two worlds: my parents' traditions and French and Canadian cultures and values.

Often when I was with my Canadian friends, I felt profoundly embarrassed by my origins. Once again my sense of belonging was split. I remember making up stories about my parents in order to protect them and myself from my friends' judgment and ridicule. I did not realize that by rejecting my parents and my origins, I was rejecting myself and I was projecting my own internalized shame on others.

In order to gain my parents' approval, I started to date a young Croatian man for a while. He was a beautiful soul, but he had the same messed-up imprints as me. We were unhappy in our respective homes, so we thought we could be happy together. We got married when he was twenty and I was eighteen. We were happy for a while. From our union came a great treasure: two beautiful children, our daughter and our son. Two beautiful souls and teachers, who came to bless our lives.

My first husband's background was similar to mine, complete with family dramas, rejection, poverty, and pain. His post-war years were spent in Germany and Belgium. In Belgium, he had graduated from the Polytechnique de Louvain. He was brilliant, a free spirit, and a talented musician and artist. He was loving and authentic with our children and taught them to have inquisitive and analytical minds. Nevertheless, we were both ill-equipped to succeed in our marriage.

Successful relationships require emotional maturity, which neither of us had. Both of us were driven by our imprints and desire to achieve the American Dream. We built a business together that would allow us to collaborate our talents. I operated an art studio in which I designed and produced stained glass and liturgical art. I was doing interior designs for churches of all denominations, and in the process, I was flirting with many gods while not trusting any. Professionally, we were on a path to success.

It was the 1960s and '70s—years of the sexual and sociocultural revolution. Values were changing rapidly. We thought we were going to change the world and truly stop war. Those were years of peace and love, of Elvis and the Beatles.

Neither my husband nor I understood the power of genetic imprints; neither did we know anything about our spiritual DNA. The days of wine and roses, romance and glamour, were progressively turning into years of tears, lies, and betrayals.

By then, the success culture, the wining and dining of clients, was taking its toll. We were both addicts/alcoholics, but we could not connect to the concept. My grandfathers had been alcoholics who would get drunk and fall down. My husband and I were drunk but falling up. We were successful. Our children were in private schools, and we had built the home of our dreams with an indoor pool and all the "success trimmings." Neither of us could subscribe to the label of being an alcoholic. We were in denial.

On many occasions, my family and my business associates complained about our drinking, both individually and as a couple. I began to set conditions with life around my drinking: I will quit when… I am happy, when the house is completed, when we get the right car, when I own the right fur coat, or after we go on the right vacation. An inner emptiness kept telling me, "You have not acquired enough; you have not accomplished enough; you are not enough; you need to have more." I was so sure that my/our life was going to be different from my parents'—it would be successful—I would achieve the true American Dream.

Then in January 1974, although we remained associated through our business, my husband left our marriage. That is when I realized I had problems. After my husband's departure, I was living in the house of my dreams and all my conditions for success had been fulfilled, yet I was more miserable than ever.

I felt lonely, defeated, humiliated, and depressed. Some of Montreal's best psychiatrists tried to help me. With my half-truths and their limited understanding of addictions, we did not get very far. My spirit was broken. I had no more drive. My health was rapidly deteriorating. My creativity and artistic talent were gone, and I had added prescription medications to my drinking. All my relationships fell apart. I was a source of shame and embarrassment to my family and associates. This period of darkness was approaching its pivotal point.

By March 1974, I had decided I could no longer go on. Life and I were done. I made the decision to die. On March 8th, a day when Canada was cold, frozen, and a lot of snow was covering the ground, I took 165 pills, and then just in case they would not be sufficient, I decided to lie outside on the porch and freeze to death.

By Divine Intervention, my son found me the next morning. When the police took me to the hospital, I had ice in my eyes and no vital signs. During this time, I had a near-death experience. First I saw my body lying on the porch, and then I went through a tunnel of light. At the other end, I was greeted by my mother who had died in 1949 and by my maternal grandfather who had died in 1953. I was taken to a place where my life was played on a screen in front of me.

When I finished watching my life story, I was taken to meet a Being of Light. In the presence of the Being of Light, I experienced an unbelievable and complete feeling of Total Peace, Total Love, and Total Acceptance. All my emotional pain and turmoil were gone. I felt truly loved, and I felt a deep compassion for myself and for all. I experienced what I can only explain as total awareness of everything.

The Being of Light told me it was not my time to die. I was told that I needed to go back, to learn a few more lessons, and that in due time a mission would be revealed. I did not want to leave that wonderful place, but I knew it was what I was meant to do.

So in 1974, after I knew I could not live, I found out that I could not die. I was left with only one alternative—to get my act together. But I had no clue how to do that. I did not then understand the depth of my depression and despair.

From March to November, I felt I was in a state of shock. My level of guilt, shame, fear, and despair was such that the only thing I knew how to do was to numb all my feelings the way I did as a child, holding my breath and simply not being present. I did not drink. I did not use medication. I was simply in a state of mental and emotional numbness. I was at the lowest point of my life.

My old imprints that "I am not good enough" and "I do not deserve love" were totally validated by my interpretation of my near-death experience: even God did not want me.

The Total Peace, Total Love, and Total Acceptance I had experienced in the presence of the Being of Light were now a distant memory. Every now and then, I would remember the feelings I'd had, and then it was like I was remembering for just a short period my true and Authentic Self. It was like a distant call to a higher truth. However, these feelings and memories would rapidly be replaced by the deep feeling of nothingness that was at the heart of my depression. Nothing had meaning in my life any longer.

My creativity, my love of art, my relationships with my family and friends were all gone. I had created a void for myself within a cocoon of loneliness.

Late in the fall of 1974, I started drinking again. I did not care any longer what happened to me, and the selfishness of my addiction prevented me from seeing what it was doing to my loved ones.

At the time, I was dating a doctor. He was the only man who never asked me to stop drinking or asked me why I was drinking. On November 25, 1974, I was at his place when he silently poured me another drink. At that moment, the film of my life played in my head. I had a déjà vu feeling. For the first time, I realized the reasons for my unhappiness and my addictions were not external but internal.

That night I knew I must transform my perceptions, behaviors, actions, and my life. When I came home, I was ready to die to all of my old ideas. I had surrendered. My battle was over and I was ready to be helped. I flushed down the toilet all my medications and drugs. I poured down the drain all the alcohol in the house. I made my first call for help. And I started to feel some peace.

7 A New Beginning

On November 27th, 1974, at thirty-six years of age, I entered into a life of recovery. I had just come through my dark night of the soul, and I could not imagine the miracles and transformations that would soon unfold.

My first few months of recovery were a time of self-loathing and guilt. I could not sleep. It was almost as if all my imprints were right in my face with all the resulting behaviors that they implied. I felt crucified between my feelings of past victimhood and my fear of the future and the unknown.

It is only when we become willing to die to our old self-defeating behaviors that love reaches us. Love touched my heart—it opened me to service. In my support group, perfect strangers understood me via their own brokenness, and together we were getting better one day at a time. They held my coffee when I was shaking; they did not judge, evaluate nor study my case; they simply understood my state of mind. They trusted me when I could not trust myself; slowly, they taught me how to trust again.

One of my mentors, a beautiful soul, undertook my spiritual education. She firmly anchored me in the transforming system of the Twelve Steps. These steps are designed to take a failure and produce a success at the other end. Physical sobriety is not the final goal but the prerequisite for a spiritual transformation. I am so grateful that I was taught, and came to believe, that relapse is not an option—only transformation is.

Forever, I will be grateful to my early teachers. Together, we were discovering every meditation and workshop possible. I was eager, ready, willing, and excited to learn and grow. The distant call to something higher was now becoming clearer and clearer for me. I fell in love with the Twelve Steps program and the idea of wellness; finally, someone was showing me how to get there.

I was told it was a spiritual program based on the spiritual principles of Honesty, Humility, Hope, Purity of Intent, and Love. Those were the principles I was to practice in all areas of my life. I could grasp that concept.

I still had a hard time with religious dogmas and the hypocrisies I had witnessed within their teachings. Then in the fall of 1975, my mentor took me to a non-denominational church where, for the first time in my life, I experienced a meditation led by a woman. She opened the meditation by saying "Beloved Father/ Mother God." Suddenly, the floodgates of my heart opened. I heard and felt the feminine aspect of God and Love. I heard my mother. I felt my innocence.

The experience made me recall the days when my artwork had led me to working with churches of all denominations. I now felt so privileged that my career had led me to meet some great mystics, beautiful professors, Carmelite and Ursuline nuns with hearts of gold, and the wonderful rabbi at Shaar Hashomayim synagogue. My imprints and fear had closed my heart to love. Now perfect Love was casting out all fear. I felt my true origin. I was remembering my Authentic Self.

That day at the meditation, I understood what Dr. Wayne Dyer meant when he said that we are spiritual beings having many human experiences. I understood my relationship with God, the Universe, and myself. In meditation, the vision of my mission (that was promised in my near-death experience) was becoming clearer. I started to have a new sense of purpose.

After that experience, my life started to come together. The deep healing of my imprints and wounds began to take place. I was truly awakening to the truth within me. I understood the spiritual principles of my program, and I started practicing them daily in all my relationships and all areas of my life. I had to apply radical forgiveness, compassion, and understanding toward myself and everyone else from my past. I started down my path away from the victimhood status I had imposed upon myself, and my days as a victimizer were seriously reduced. I was making progress.

I was falling in love with my life. I saw possibilities, and I was gaining a sense of oneness. When the Inner Reality changes, outer circumstances change too. In January of 1976, my first husband and I went to court for the first hearing of our divorce. You do not end eighteen years of marriage that include two children and owning a business together without feeling the pain. We were both crying, yet we knew it was the right decision for both of us.

I felt supported, guided, and protected. I was two years sober and recovering. Unfortunately, my ex-husband was not. Addictions kill. In December 1976, at the age of forty, my ex-husband died of alcoholism, although the death certificate said cardiac arrest. He was a brilliant, sweet man who could not surrender. Addictions are deadly; either we surrender or they break us.

His death really made me pay attention to what was next for me. What would I do with the rest of my life—what was my calling? I sold my shares of the company and took a sabbatical. I knew I wanted to serve and make a difference. I knew that the greatest amends I could make to all those I loved would be a profound change of personality.

One of my hardest challenges when I entered recovery was that my first five years I lived alone. *My imprint was: My value is defined by a man and marriage.* Therefore, I perceived living alone as a sign of failure that left me feeling lonely.

Today, however, I know that time was necessary to my healing process; it allowed me to discover my inner strengths and to rewrite the script of my relationships. It was a period of intense healing as I tried to figure out my purpose in life.

When we set a clear intention, miracles start happening and life takes us at our word. One day I drove a friend to a treatment at the first private rehab center in Quebec, Pavillon Pointe du Saule. It had been started by one of my friends, so soon I was asked to consider volunteering there. I accepted and immediately fell in love with the program.

As my involvement with the rehab center increased, I decided to be trained to work in the field of addictions. For three years, I was a full-time volunteer. From this phase of my life came my new calling—my mission and profession.

The founder of Pavillon Pointe du Saule was a charming Frenchman named Gilles Desjardins. I respected his work and learned a lot from him. We became colleagues and best friends. In 1978, we discovered we were soul mates, and in July 1979, we got married.

Our mentor performed the wedding ceremony for us. We were married at the Sheraton Waikiki in Hawaii, overlooking the ocean and Diamond Head. It was beautiful, sacred, and romantic. Our mentor told us that we truly saw each other through the eyes of God because we looked at each other through the eyes of love. He also said that we should leave our past on the bottom of the Hawaiian ocean. Certainly that was our intent.

Having had previous marriages, both my husband and I wanted to build the "Us" space, the space of partnership instead of the codependent enmeshments of our previous relationships. Our intention was clear—to be united in a bigger purpose. We had both done extensive inner work and healing. Now we felt ready to embark on the path of sacred partnership. After an unforgettable honeymoon in Hawaii, we returned to Montreal and our joint adventure—the Pavillon.

As Canadian citizens, our Hawaiian wedding was not official in Canada, so we chose March 1980 for a Canadian ceremony.

From July 1979 to March 1980, I slowly became reluctant to be officially married. I could not understand why. I was having strange fear attacks that I knew had nothing to do with my husband; he was a great guy.

Yet I was unhappy, restless, and I could not commit. It got to the point where I had to close myself up for three days in a downtown hotel and write a big inventory of my beliefs. What I discovered was that all of my imprints and beliefs about men, women, love, sex, and marriage I had received from my mother, stepmother, grandmother, and all the women before me.

Some of my imprints and beliefs about marriage belonged to Balkan culture, some to French culture, and some to the Catholic Church. I will talk more about those beliefs later in this book. What was important for me to realize was that none of those beliefs corresponded to my personal values or my intellectual perceptions of marriage and relationships with the opposite sex.

Once I had this realization, I went home. My husband and I then established together our mutual vision, beliefs, and values for our marriage. I felt a sense of peace and belonging that never left me. Together, we redefined our vocabulary by removing the emotional trigger words, name calling, comparisons, put downs, and other words and phrases that were detrimental to building a trusting relationship. We took out the word "divorce" and replaced it with "commitment" and "willingness to resolve conflicts."

Once I stopped being an opponent to my husband and stopped perceiving him as the enemy, I started being a friend, his best friend. Instead of expecting and waiting for the other shoe to drop, I started giving unconditionally. Instead of demanding, I started allowing. Instead of looking at my husband through the eyes of my parents—checking everything that is wrong and not perfect—I started seeing the blessings and the goodness in him.

One of the transformed Imprints for both of us was the switch from the hierarchical model of relationships (where one is superior and the other inferior; one is co-dependent and the other is counter-dependent) to a synergistic partnership. The synergistic partnership capitalizes on the partners' differences and empowers both of them to be more. There is me, there is him, but there is the greater unit called "US." Both of us made the commitment to invest the best of us into this sacred unit called US.

Little did we know what a wonderful adventure lay before us as a married couple and team. Our joint passion for treatment, wellness, and human beings took us through many different phases of challenges, growth, and victories.

At that time, the United States was making great progress in the field of addictions while in Quebec addiction was still being viewed as a sin or as a moral issue. The American Medical Association recognized addiction as a disease. Gilles and I decided we needed to go to the United States for training since that's where our role models were. As a result, Pavillon Pointe du Saule was transformed from a dry-out place for alcoholics and drug addicts into a rehabilitation center.

Working with the families of alcoholics and drug addicts, we came to realize how addictions were a family disease because they affected the entire family. Soon we started to include spouses and adult children of alcoholics in the group program. We were fortunate also to work with very progressive organizations that understood the need for family treatment. LaBatt and Molson breweries were the forerunners when their employee assistance programs agreed to pay for family treatment. Soon General Motors of Canada's Ste. Therese plant, and then many others followed.

Suddenly, we had a very organic group promoting much deeper understanding, compassion, and forgiveness. Addicts began to understand how their diseases affected their spouses and children. Spouses started to understand the emotional make-up of addictions, and they came to recognize how the addict's behavior had created co-addict characteristics within them. Family treatments allowed everyone to understand the devastating process of addictions.

Witnessing these dynamics, we intuitively knew that we needed to change our model into a closed group model where the entire group started on the same day and ended on the same day. Wow! That change resulted in the group's trust level increasing. Therapeutic alliances were formed. Empathy, motivation, and support among clients skyrocketed. Clients stayed in touch for years after treatment. They became their best support system since they truly knew and supported one another.

In 1983, Pavillon Pointe du Saule became Pavillon Gilles Desjardins. We shifted from a French-speaking facility to an English-speaking facility with the majority of our clients coming from the United States. Pavillon became a treatment facility for addictions and compulsive behaviors and an organic laboratory for the study of human behaviors. Our focus became not only addictions, but the essence of human pain.

It did not take long to realize that substance addictions were simply the tip of the iceberg: the visible part of the problem. Beneath the surface were all the process addictions: co-dependency, relationship addiction, workaholism, food addiction, sex addiction, gambling, shopping addiction, and Internet addiction. These behaviors were all psychological medicators for the pain that lay beneath the surface.

Why are they called process addictions? Because you have to learn to live with and manage them. You need a life management system to do that. Substance addictions require the individual to stop, quit, and not use. Once the individual has done that, he/she needs to learn how to deal with life sober. Process addictions on the other hand have a different requirement for recovery. The addict continues to eat, work, or have sex; therefore, he/she must learn a life management system in order to manage these addictions.

Through our work with both substance and process addictions, we noticed a common denominator to all addictions which are called the "Core Addictions." The four Core Addictions are: Security Addiction, or the Not Enough Syndrome; Power and Control Addiction; Sensation Addiction; and Addiction to Suffering.

Once we realized that Core Addictions were the link in the Addiction Interaction Disorder, the Desjardins Unified Model of Addictions was born.

What we learned will be shared in the second part of this book, which includes stories from some of our clients and friends who have made the journey to recovery and tools you can find to overcome your own negative imprints. It is my hope that this information will allow you to overcome your own negative imprints and begin the transformation to finding your Authentic Self.

Part II -

Tools For Your Imprint Journey

8 Going Inward--Going Deeper

The Desjardins Unified Model assumes that substance and process addictions are progressive illnesses, the manifestations of a disease that affects the biological, psychological, social, and spiritual aspects of a client. A client's genetic make-up can predispose him/her toward substance or process addiction. However, the environment plays a crucial role in either triggering the predisposition toward addiction or keeping it latent. A client's neurobiology determines his/her proclivity for one substance addiction as opposed to another.

Furthermore, the model postulates a comprehensive definition of addiction under the umbrella of "Addiction Interaction Disorder."

Addiction Interaction Disorder addresses the appearance of another addiction after a recognized addiction has been treated, and it explains how one addiction is used to trigger another. The core pathology is an abnormal and dysfunctional craving for security, for power/control, sensations, and suffering—the four Core Addictions.

Core Addictions themselves interrelate. The addiction to security, which develops as a result of fear-based childhood emotional imprints, when a person is neither mentally nor physically mature enough to discern for him or herself, is often sustained by the belief that there is never enough love, resources, people, money, things, etc. Most importantly the person has integrated the belief that he or she is "not enough," which in turn fosters a deep sense of shame, leaving the person feeling fundamentally defective.

This unbearable belief about the self is then switched into a power/control addiction as a compensating mechanism or into a sensation addiction to numb the devastating feelings about self. Regardless of how it is switched, it will end in the addiction to suffering. Within the four Core Addictions lie the primary motivating forces fueling either or both process and substance addictions.

At Pavillon, we learned that for our clients to have lasting results in their recovery and treatment, we needed to help them become aware of their self-perceptions and shift from an identification with "ego" (addict-self) to an identification with "identity" (true self/Authentic Self).

Ego is defined as: "A distortion in the perception of the self created by an adherence to fear-based paradigms. The *Ego* identifies with external values and is reactive in nature."

In our model, *Ego* is the negative self: negative beliefs and imprints, negative self-perception and self-esteem, as well as negative self-image and self-worth. It is also the negative and/or addictive attitudes and behaviors, and the self-limiting and self-destructive patterns and character defects. *Ego* perpetuates denial and is rooted in the unrealistic notion of control.

Identity is defined as: "The spiritual-based Self that identifies with inner values of Truth and Love and is Proactive in nature. The Identity is the Authentic Self, which is positive and creative."

Identity is the Positive Self: Positive beliefs and imprints, positive self-perceptions, positive self-esteem, positive self-image and self-worth. *Identity* is also the positive and empowering attitudes, behaviors, creative and constructive patterns, strengths, skills, and talents. *Identity* is based in truth and compassion; it is flexible, it co-operates, and it co-creates.

Working with this model produced some great results; lives were transformed. We moved beyond focusing solely on clients who had addictions to including clients who had no identifiable addiction but were in pain due to the death of a loved one, a divorce, a job loss, early retirement—simply, people who were dealing with pain in their lives.

One common denominator in their pain was their imprints—their deep-seated perceptions and beliefs about life, death, God, self, and others.

In this sacred laboratory called Pavillon, we were given the privilege to study, monitor, and understand the dynamics created by imprints. We worked with people from all walks of life who came to us from all continents. The mission I had been promised had now become a reality. I had found—we had found—our Higher Purpose.

Imprints shape people's reality as well as their behavior. Behavior affects four levels of our being: thinking, feeling, doing, and physiologizing. Physiologizing means that whatever we do not deal with consciously will cause our physiology to react to it. For example, when you are caught in a lie, you blush because your body is dealing with your suppressed feelings of fear and/or shame.

Since my retirement from active clinical duties, I have fully concentrated my professional work on helping individuals gain freedom from their self-limiting imprints and beliefs, and thereby helping them to get in touch with their inner hidden potential and genius—their true Authentic Self.

Imprints, as a subconscious emotional map, affect our thinking, our feelings, and our behaviors. In the following chapters, I will illustrate further how they work.

9 Anatomy of an Imprint

In this chapter, I will focus on *Negative Imprints:* their origin, development, effects, key areas, and core questions to identify the imprints. To facilitate the understanding and impact of imprints, I will also share my family imprints as well as case studies.

Imprints are...

- ...our deep-seated beliefs.
- ...the subconscious motive for our behavior and our choices.
- ...our emotional map and they contain our value system.
- ...the determining factor in our ability to relate to others.
- ...our genetic encoding.
- ...the internalized environmental/familial messages we receive.

Origin of Imprints:

GENETIC IMPRINTS: "Introduction to Genetics" in Wikipedia describes *genetics* as the study of genes, and tries to explain what they are and how they work. Genes are how living organisms inherit features from their ancestors; for example, children usually look like their parents because they have inherited their parents' genes. Genetics tries to identify which features are inherited, and explain how these features are passed from generation to generation. In biology, and specifically genetics, *epigenetics* is the study of inherited changes in appearance or gene expression caused by mechanisms other than changes in the underlying DNA sequence. The way our genes and environment interact to produce a trait can be complicated. For example, the chances of somebody dying of cancer or heart disease seems to depend on both the person's genes and his or her lifestyle.

The areas in which genetic imprints are most vivid are:

- Physical resemblance to a parent
- Certain mannerisms

- Predisposition to certain illnesses: addictions, heart disease, cancer, although as previously stated these can also be greatly influenced by the environment

ENVIRONMENTAL IMPRINTS: Are all the internalized cultural/societal/religious/peer messages received in early childhood. Some examples:

- Physical, mental, emotional, sexual, religious abuse is acceptable but needs to be hidden

- We live in a world of scarcity and lack

- You're a sinner; God will punish you; you will burn in Hell

- Only our religion is the right one; people of other faiths are evil and will go to Hell

- Immigrants and those who are different from us are evil

- We are the superior race, others (blacks, Hispanics, etc.) are inferior

- Women are inferior to men

FAMILIAL IMPRINTS: Are all the internalized messages received from our family of origin, and/or adoptive and extended family. Some examples are:

- You are not good enough; you must be perfect

- You are an extension and reflection of you parents; therefore, don't shame us

- You're bad; you're stupid; you're a burden

- People are out to get you....do not trust others

- There is not enough money; money does not grow on trees

- You are not lucky

- You are what you have; your possessions define you

- You are what you do; your accomplishments and your monetary success define you

- You are what others think of you; your reputation defines you

- Happiness comes from others

KEY IMPRINT AREAS: When identifying imprints, it is important to zero in on the key area where you might be experiencing repetitive problems. To avoid confusion, work with one area at a time. The key areas are:

- Love/Relationships/Family

- Health

- Financial

- Religious/Spiritual
- Educational
- Social
- Life Purpose/Success

CORE QUESTIONS: When identifying an imprint in key areas, ask yourself:

- What is the negative role modeling you have received growing up in the above areas?
- What were the negative (spoken and unspoken) messages you have received from Family, Educators, Religion, Society, Peers?
- How have you internalized these messages?
- What is your perception and deep-seated belief/imprint regarding the received messages?
- To your knowledge, is the imprint one carried over from one generation to the other?
- Which of your behaviors are still triggered by this belief/imprint?
- What difficulties is your belief/imprint causing now in your life?
- Is the difficulty persisting in spite of different efforts to change it?

EXAMPLE: If your chosen area is finances, because you are repeatedly experiencing financial lack or difficulties, ask yourself the following important sub-questions:

- What kind of relationship do you have with money?
- Do you struggle with money...how and why?
- Do you feel unworthy of it...if yes, why?
- What is your perception of money?
- What are the negative messages and role modeling you have received in your childhood about money?
- What is your deep-seated belief/imprint about money?
- How did you acquire this belief/imprint?
- How did your father handle money? What kind of relationship did he have with money?
- How did your mother handle money? What kind of relationship did she have with money?
- What are the negative messages you have received from your educators regarding money?

- What were the religious messages you have received regarding money?
- What were society's messages you have received regarding money?
- What do you believe is your imprint regarding money?
- What is your perception of Abundance?
- What is your deep belief/imprint about Abundance?
- What is your relationship and personal experience with Abundance?
- Who and what is the Source of all your Good?

Personal Examples:

IN MY FAMILY OF ORIGIN AREA, time was a very important factor.
My mother was always busy and had no time for me.
My father was busy or gone and had no time for me.
I have internalized their lack of time as:

- I am not good enough.
- People don't want to be with me.
- I am not worthy of their time.
- Time is presence; presence is love.
- I am not lovable.

For years if I needed something from someone, I would always preface my request with "I am sorry to trouble you" even if I were doing the person a favor.

I had no intellectual boundaries; if I came to you with a great idea, but you looked at your watch, my idea disappeared, and I felt not good enough nor worthy of your time.

My self-esteem was tied into other people's time management. I had to learn an appropriate sense of timing as I was learning to defuse the emotional energy of my imprints.

IN MY HEALTH AREA, food was a great factor.
My dad's role modeling, messages, and rules about food and eating were:

- There's not enough food, we don't waste food, you must eat all that is on your plate = not enough and scarcity.
- Tomorrow there might not be any food = fear and hoarding.
- There are people starving and you do not want to eat; shame on you = guilt and shame.

If I did not like something or could not eat, my dad forced me until I would get sick.

My negative imprints regarding food were:

- Lack and not enough
- Punishment and Fear

For years, I ate as fast as possible to get away from the table. I hardly chewed my food and gulped it down, without tasting it, in order to avoid tasting food that was distasteful to me.

On the other hand, my mother, even in the hard times of war when food was scarce, had a great talent for preparing wonderful little treats and serving them in a loving way. She was a great hostess, and my mother's view of food was a family gathering, a beautifully set table, and friendly conversation.

I was split between my parents and developed a love-hate relationship with food, as well as an eating disorder that varied between overeating, anorexia, and bulimia. It took recovery to change these imprints and behaviors.

In My Financial and Educational Areas

My father came from poverty and great depression. His role modeling was Fear, Insecurity, Lack, and Not Enough Money.

My father's main message about money was that money does not grow on trees and you must work very hard for it. Other messages were:

- You must hide your money and be secretive about it because others can and will take it away from you.
- Don't trust.
- You must have a practical job; art and education are a loss of time; they will not feed you.
- You don't know how to handle money; you will squander everything.
- You must save and deprive yourself…you never know what will happen.
- We don't need that…who do you think you are?
- Men handle money.
- You must have financial integrity and pay your bills.

My mother came from a middle class family where education and creativity were important and defined you. She was raised to earn money, and even in hard times of war, she was working and producing an income. She was not preoccupied with savings, but with making the money and doing creative things with it.

These opposite role models and messages have shaped my perception of money as well as my relationship with money.

For years if I bought something for myself, I felt guilty, as if I were squandering. If I did not buy it, I felt deprived and punished while fearing lack of money.

Yet at the same time, like my mother, I have worked all my life. I have produced money and was always involved in very creative work. I was involved in liturgical arts, yet felt guilty about it because it was fun and not hard work, and therefore, not productive according to my father's message. Like my father, I have financial integrity and pay my bills on time.

For years, my relationship with money was a love hate relationship: I would make it and spend it and then feared not having it.

So let's take a look at how the messages are internalized and turned into imprints affecting behavior at all levels. Behavior works at four levels: Thinking, Feeling, Doing and Physiologizing (if we do not deal consciously with stress, our body will deal with it).

Some Messages I Received From My Parents:

I don't have time for you...I am busy, I have to work...there's not enough money nor security...don't trust anyone...you're making your mother cry...it's your fault...you should be ashamed...we're not lucky...money does not grow on trees...you squander everything.

BEHAVIOR

THINKING: (How I handled my imprints intellectually):
I know my parents are good people and they did the best they could...i am just fine...I'll fake it till I make it...I don't need anyone...I can do it by myself...i don't need help...I don't need their love...the purpose of life is to work very hard...to have value, you must produce and make money.

FEELING: (How I handled it at the feeling level):
I feel insecure, inadequate, flawed, different, ashamed, not smart enough, not pretty enough, not intelligent enough, not successful enough, not rich enough. I am fearful, I worry, I feel guilty and self-centered. I feel neglected, rejected, hurt, and abandoned. I feel responsible for people's feelings. I am envious of other people's "luck/success."

DOING/ACTION: (How I reacted and behaved):
I people please and care take, I am co-dependent, I need your approval, I cling to people, I don't rock the boat. I can't stand confrontation nor conflict. I attract emotionally unavailable people who do not have time for me, thus I feel rejected, abandoned, and isolated. My security addiction and addiction to suffering are turned on. I am in power struggles, I compete, I control, I prove, I fight, I argue. I work hard. I am a human doing. I have to succeed more and acquire more. I am a perfectionist with very high expectations. I blame, I resent, I judge and reject. Power/control addiction and sensation addiction are turned on. I have to medicate my feelings: sex/food/relationships/shopping/substances—I will use anything that will numb the battle between my thoughts and feelings.

These examples illustrate how imprints get internalized and turned into deep belief systems and perceptions. Let me elaborate more by giving you my parent's negative imprints.

It has taken me a lot of self-awareness, clearing, and cleansing of my own imprints to get to the point of understanding my parents' imprints with a compassionate heart.

My Father's Negative Imprints:

To Be Responsible Meant	To worry a lot To fear the worst-case scenario To have an eye for all the errors To be secretive about finances To trust no one To control others and his environment
His Imprint of Love	To worry for those you love means you care To pay bills and provide To tell you what is wrong with you Love is conditional and must be earned Love is sex
His Imprint of Sex	Sex is Power and a man's right Sex is the chase Sex is not to be discussed in the family
His Imprint of Happiness	Happiness is having control over others Happiness is to be obeyed Happiness is absence of worry; therefore Happiness is Unattainable Happiness is having money in the bank Happiness is hunting and fishing
His Imprint of Women	Women are wives, cooks, maids, and mothers Women are second-class citizens If young and pretty, women are objects for attention and desire = sex objects There are two categories of women: those you marry and those with whom you have fun
His Imprint of Marriage	Marriage is a trap, a prison, a burden, a status You have to do it: kids need a mother
His Imprint of Money	There is not enough of it Money does not grow on trees; it is hard to get Don't trust anyone with it Money is Power, Status, and Freedom

My Mother's Negative Imprints:

Her Imprint of Men	Men are selfish, immature, irresponsible; you can't count on them Men are necessary and they define you Men have to be taken care of Men cheat on you and betray you; they make you cry Men are controlling and not good enough
Her Imprint of Women	Women are strong, caretakers, fixers, and preachers Women are controlling, demanding, and blaming Women are victimized, naïve, gullible, and dependent Women are not good enough
Her Imprint of Love	To love is to worry, care take, people-please Work, work, work! Love is to deny one's needs To love is to check and control Love is conditional and punishing Love does not last and disappoints you Love is tears, suffering, and sadness There is not enough love
Her Imprint of Marriage	Marriage is a trap, a prison, a loss of self, hard work Marriage is a loss of freedom
Her Imprint of Sex	Fear of getting pregnant Duty and a chore A hidden subject and a hidden agenda Sadness and loneliness Unfaithfulness and betrayal
Her Imprint Of Happiness	To be happy is to have all work done, which never happens; therefore, is unattainable Happiness is a present, loving, faithful husband; again non-existent Happiness is all expectations fulfilled; does not happen Happiness is an illusion

My parents inherited their negative imprints from their parents, society, and religion. Their imprints were greatly influenced by the family disease of alcoholism, which was never identified nor treated. My parents did not know that they could change their imprints.

My parents internalized the shame, unworthiness, and the inadequacy of their disease. In their day, addictions were viewed as a sin, a moral degradation, even sometimes the result of being possessed by demons or the devil. Like most people, my parents were unaware of their imprints. When the war and other traumatic life events happened, it magnified the impact of these imprints upon them.

How I understand today my parents' fears and pain, their worries, doubts, and shame. They were brave souls who, despite their circumstances, managed to do so much with so little. My mom died at thirty-six years of age from cancer. Suppressed and repressed feelings become depressed feelings and our physiology responds with illness as it did in my mother's case. My dad, however, passed away in 2003 at the age of ninety-five. I am so grateful for the gift of my biological life. I am grateful to have known these two brave children. Emotionally they were not very old, yet both possessed extraordinary strengths and survival skills.

Later, I will discuss the positive imprints my parents gave me. In spite of all the pain in my parents' lives, I have known the sweetness of their spirits and the generosity of their hearts. This book is about re-writing the generational script of our family, our lives, not just my own but hopefully also yours.

I have a much deeper appreciation for my parents when I consider what they were given as a result of the social, cultural, and religious contexts of their time. Religion and politics were intertwined and enmeshed. The church still ruled and set the moral standards, to which, in many cases, it did not adhere, thereby adding to the erosion of values and the lack of decency and dignity brought by two world wars.

It was a time of confusion when there was a mass consciousness of darkness. The twentieth century and the beginning of the twenty-first brought the worst of humanity to the surface, but in doing so, the hypocrisy of the time's systems were exposed.

Wars fought in the name of God, where the end justifies the means, are based in pure ego. Genocide, ethnic cleansing, destruction of civilizations for the profit of the "Super Powers," is pure ego and the core Power/Control addiction in action. When these acts are justified in the name of religion and God, the minds of children and future generations are poisoned with imprints of fear and hatred.

The hierarchical systems of exploitation and domination then permeate the entire society until socio-economic structures reflect these imprints. For centuries, the victims of these systems were made to believe that their salvation would come in Heaven while the victimizers were allowed to continue exploitation and domination by cultivating the dependence of the masses on the Powers/Authorities of Church and State.

For many people, the process of becoming and maturing into the Authentic Self is painful and slow. Only now are we starting to understand the power of the mind, the plasticity of our brains, and our ability to change and transform. We are breaking the new frontier and starting to conquer our minds.

Needless to say, my parent's negative imprints greatly influenced my own. So here are some of my early imprints.

My Self-Perception:	I am not enough I am what I do and what I have I am what others think of me I am flawed and damaged
My Resulting Behavior	I work hard to prove my worthiness I control and compete I people please
My Imprint Of Love	Does not last What I love goes away and I am abandoned Love is conditional and cannot be trusted Love is doubt, worry, and pain
My Resulting Behavior	I cling to people/depend on them I settle for crumbs I avoid and I isolate I smother and control
My Perception Of Marriage	Marriage does not work Marriage is loss of self Marriage is pain and crying Marriage is a burden Marriage is secrets, lies, and betrayals Marriage is money and power struggles
My Resulting Behavior	I fight, argue, compete, comply I leave emotionally, I reject
My Perception Of Men	They are unfair, immature, selfish, and self-centered They don't show up when you need them They are bossy, controlling, and cheating They are male chauvinists, macho men They are not good enough

My Resulting Behavior	I must control them, raise them, correct them, manipulate them, people please with them, buy peace with them
My Perception Of Women	Second-class citizens, not good enough A maid, a cook, a mother, a nurse, a victim A woman has to do everything Is inferior to men and must ask permission Must hide her intelligence, strength, and feelings
My Resulting Behavior	Be a human doing Control everything Suffer, put up with it Complain or nag But don't rock the boat
My Perception Of Life	It is a struggle, it is hard, it is dangerous It is full of disappointments It is a half-empty glass You never know...the worst can happen Life is suffering and the way to Heaven is paved with pain; bear your cross Others have the power to take away what is mine
My Resulting Behavior:	Defensive living in victimhood
My Perception Of Happiness:	It comes from outside It is supposed to be provided by a man It is unattainable It could happen if I am perfect enough It is conditional to my success and possessions
My Resulting Behavior:	I wait and procrastinate I have high expectations and end up disappointed; thereby I can continue my belief of not enough and of being victimized

One of the truly painful and problematic imprints throughout my life has been my body image, which is basically as follows:

My Perception Of My Body:	I am my body; my body defines me My body does not belong to me it belongs to a man: he has the power to validate or reject it Is a source of pain Is a source of shame: at six years of age, I was taught to be ashamed of my body, never to touch it, and never to let anyone else touch it. Family, church, and society's double and puritanical standards perpetuated this image Is source of strength: for survival and hard work, tired or aching, it was made for endurance Is a baby making factory, where you have no choice, no rights, no say, all in the name of God, church, and state Is source of food for babies. I felt guilty due to my difficulty breast-feeding my children Is source of pleasure for man…the way to keep him Is source of illegal pleasure Large breasts are a prerequisite to being loved and desired Must be thin and petite, and of value only if wanted and desired sexually by a man
Body With Age	To be hidden, neglected, ignored Source of aches and pain Drooping Once again, point of shame and self-rejection
Fat Body	Guarantee to stay faithful (like a chastity belt Fat body is self-protection; it is a wall against rejection. Body needs to be numbed with food to avoid feeling fear, rejection, etc.

The body imprints I received from French culture, while living in Paris, totally clashed with my Slavic imprints and created even more confusion.

My French Imprint of Body:	The female body is to be pampered, massaged, shaped, exhibited The female body is super-feminine, coquettish, seductive, sexy, beautiful, promiscuous (prostitution is legal, open and visible The body is self-indulgence; it is youth, cosmetic surgery, and hedonistic values

Because I could never fit into any of these images of what the body should be, I have spent a good portion of my life not wanting to be in my body, but still having to put up with it. I went from starving my body to episodes of bulimia and overeating, then back to starving, and neglecting it, to acting out sexually to be noticed, and then being sexually anorexic. I was self-rejecting, abandoning myself and abusing my body.

We can be very advanced in certain areas of our lives and have total blind spots in others. The healing of my body image was one of the transformational points in my life. By adjusting to seeing my body as a wonderful spacesuit in which my spirit resides, I have found new self-love, peace, and freedom.

All of the previously listed imprints were my blueprint for happiness and success in my life. Today, I know my extreme experiences were all needed as part of my mission and purpose. Nevertheless, the first part of my life was played according to this script.

Now I can hear you thinking, "Yes, but those are your imprints; my experiences are not the same—I didn't live during the war, I never went to Paris. No one in my family has any addictions." You are right; my experiences are not the same as yours. However, let me give you a few more illustrations for how you can apply my and other people's stories and realizations to your own life.

As I said previously, by working in a clinical setting for so many years, my husband and I came to realize how imprints impact people's lives even if they have no identified addictions or compulsive behaviors. We have worked with people from all walks of life who have displayed the power of negative imprints in their lives.

Assimilated familial, cultural, and emotional imprinting creates repetitive patterns that are self-defeating. The assimilated cultural imprints form habits, morals, unspoken rules, and values that often create abuse, control, mistrust, and perfectionism, which are the true poisons of happiness.

Years ago, I worked with a woman named Elizabeth who came from a well-educated background; her father was a medical doctor and her mother was a college professor, both ambitious and successful people with high achievement standards and expectations. Elizabeth was the oldest of three children. She was a professional woman who belonged to the right club and the right church. She was a very well established and respected woman. However, she was unhappy, hardly ever satisfied, working very hard, and yet somehow sabotaging and limiting her possibilities. She came to us on a burnout.

Elizabeth's Negative Imprints And Self-Perception:

I Am What I Do And Have	But it is not enough; I have not done enough
	I don't have enough: money, time, diplomas, recognition
	I don't measure up to my parents' expectations
Her Religious Imprint	I am separate from God, I am just a
	sinner, not good enough, undeserving

With these two imprints, she was perpetually trying to achieve self-worth through perfectionism, people pleasing, approval seeking, and a deep sense that no matter how much she had done, how much she had was *not enough*.

The only way she knew how to compensate was through more work, more accomplishments, more diplomas, more possessions, until she crashed, overwhelmed and overworked.

It was beautiful to watch Elizabeth's transformation. As she got in touch with her Authentic Self and her Divine Imprint, she truly surrendered the old beliefs that served her no longer. She updated her relationship with God and with herself, and she chose a new set of values for her life.

Another example is Frank, who was a brilliant intellect. He had two Ph.D.'s and two Master degrees. He was a true treasure of knowledge. His only problem: he did not "do people." He had a few unsuccessful marriages and very stressful professional relationships. He could not understand why. He was very religious. He knew about God, but he did not trust nor experience God. To experience God required the willingness and ability to be vulnerable, humble, and open to love. Frank's imprints said: *I would rather be right than happy*. To be right and prove we are right boosts the ego and paralyzes our Authentic Self. Frank had to take the trip from his head into his heart. How precious it was to witness his surrender as he embraced his own vulnerability and innocence. Love and wisdom combined are powerful!

We also worked with Bradley. Bradley came from a large family. His mother died when he was young so he did not receive any nurturing. His father was uneducated, strict, demanding, and physically abusive. Bradley became the protector of his younger siblings. He swore he would get them out of this abusive situation and the family's poverty. Rather than pursue education, he put all of his energy into becoming a powerful and successful businessman. He was a blue-collar worker who climbed his way up the ladder and into the boardroom of a large corporation to become the CEO of a Fortune 500 company. Bradley had spent his life being a caretaker, enabler, fixer, and provider for everyone around him. With a heart of gold and generosity without limits, he had done so much for so many. However, he had no perception of his own greatness. His ego kept fighting the imprints of Not Enough and Inadequacy, and the only way Bradley knew how to cope with these imprints was through the Power/Control and Sensations addictions. Because Bradley could not learn to surrender, in the end the addictions killed him.

Pierre was another powerful and successful man who came to Pavillon. Despite belonging to a very wealthy family, he too was stuck with the imprint of Not Enough. Although he was the head of a family fortune worth billions, Pierre would experience fear attacks where he would cancel and cut up all the credit cards, and then he would go into isolation. His family and associates greatly resented his financial control and panic attacks. They could not understand why he was acting that way. Pierre could not understand either. He came to understand that because his father had survived the Great Depression, his father had passed onto him imprints about money and success that were imprinted with the fear and panic of the times. Although Pierre's family made its fortune after the Great Depression, the imprints of Lack, Scarcity, and Not Enough were still there. Pierre's financial control destroyed his marriage and finally brought him into treatment. While in treatment, Pierre realized that money was a false god. He got in touch with his workaholism, shopping addiction, and of course, his core addictions. His divorce was finalized. However, through his recovery, Pierre has rebuilt his life. Today, he is happily married, has a good relationship with his children, and is enjoying his retirement free from fear.

Michael came to us depressed. He had been in therapy for years, but nothing seemed to work. He had chronic sadness, and he was desperate for help. As we worked with him, we discovered that his parents were survivors of the Holocaust. His imprints were deep and powerful. Michael had internalized his parents' suffering and the survivor guilt. *His imprints were: I have no right to happiness, peace, joy, and love. I must suffer and perpetuate the suffering to keep the memory alive.* His suffering was manifested through a series of bad and difficult relationships and financial setbacks. Carrying such an imprint, coupled with the religious and cultural imprint of belonging to a chosen/persecuted people, is a heavy burden for a man to carry. It took Michael a lot of inner work, courage, and faith to change his imprint without feeling like a traitor so he could overcome his depression. In Dr. Judith Orloff's *Emotional Freedom*, she refers to depression as the "Dark Night of the Soul," an assessment with which I agree. In treatment, Michael found his True Self as well as his calling/mission. He now works with children of war, helping them heal, forgive, and regain hope.

We have worked with Native Americans, stuck between their conflicting imprints of a pride in their ancestors and their connectedness to Mother Earth and their misguided beliefs that they are a subculture, inferior, inadequate, and dominated. The powerlessness experienced keeps many in inertia. One Native American client was Johnny. He was an artist, a sensitive and beautiful soul. His father was a prominent man in their tribe, and Johnny was raised to succeed; however, his imprints continued to sabotage his potential success. Despite his talent, in a world of white artists he felt inferior. *His imprint said: You're a second-class citizen. You're inferior; you have no rights.* He worked very hard, pushed, controlled, medicated his feelings, and killed his art. Only after Johnny realized his true origin and touched the beauty of his soul was he capable of blossoming. Another Native American client I will never forget is Yavapai, the chief and religious leader of a well-known tribe. Yavapai found freedom when he managed to reconnect to his true essence. Standing in all the beauty of his regalia, he said, "All my life I've been trained to be a chief. Now I know how to be an Indian."

At Pavillon, we have also worked with the gay and lesbian community. Wow! How powerful were their imprints of rejection, of being flawed, and being a disgrace. Deep depression, suicide attempts, and/or addictions usually brought them to us. One gay man, Steven, came to us with a broken spirit. He had been demonized, exorcized, and dragged through processes that were supposed to eliminate his "vice." *His imprint was: I am not normal. I am possessed by evil spirits; I am vicious; God does not love me; I will burn in Hell.* Steven was dragged from church to church, and with every experience, he was sinking lower in his self-esteem. Steven's imprints were making him sabotage every area of his life because he had a deep feeling that he did not deserve to be loved, accepted, respected, nor successful. With the inner work Steven has done, he's a joy to behold. He has blossomed. He has dedicated his life to helping the gay community.

The true purpose of life for all of us is to be who we are designed to be; that requires freedom from the illusions and false perceptions formed by our negative imprints. I am continually amazed by the healing power of love and what happens to an individual via forgiveness, compassion, and a shift in self-perception.

From the time Martha was eight years old until she was eighteen, her father sexually and emotionally abused her. All of Martha's boundaries were broken. *Her imprint was: There is no safety; my body does not belong to me; I am his prisoner; I am trash, I do not deserve love. There is no God. No one is there for me, and Love is abuse.* Martha's father made her believe that no one else could love her; only he loved her. He made her believe that sex is love and that she deserved abuse. He made her believe that he would kill her and her mother if she revealed their secret. A few times, Martha tried to run away, but because her father was a prominent man in the community, the police always brought her back home. *Her other imprint was: I can't trust anyone, I am alone and a victim, I am my pain.* Martha repressed her anger and rage; she turned them into self-hatred and self-loathing. Through a series of fortunate circumstances, loving people helped Martha to get out of the house and into treatment. Martha could not talk. She was consumed by toxic shame. But love is the greatest healer in the world. Mature, selfless love allows people to heal. As she began to realize she had people who loved her, Martha started responding. Her miracle was reclaiming her innocence, forgiving, and letting go. Because forgiveness is an act of self-love, it is the key to our freedom. Martha was and is a very intelligent and bright young lady. Once she touched the beauty and purity of her Spirit, she soared into a brilliant career. Today, Martha is a beautiful woman who makes a great difference in the world. Out of her pain was born a deep compassion and understanding for self and others.

Unfortunately, many victims of sexual abuse end up being sexual addicts. At Pavillon, we worked with many victims of sexual abuse and sex addicts. For centuries, sex addiction was called "womanizing" and was considered a fact of life. In other cases, it was hidden and never addressed. In many cultures, it remains a sign of manhood, of status and rights.

As we started understanding addictive processes, and as the Internet brought cybersex into being, sex addiction became recognized. The term "Sex Addiction" is used to describe the behavior of a person who has an unusually intense sex drive or an obsession with either having or avoiding sex. Sexual acts and thoughts tend to dominate the sex addict's behavior, making it difficult for him or her to engage in healthy personal relationships. As with any other addiction, sex addicts engage in dishonest thinking, rationalizing, justifying, and excusing their behaviors. Dr. Patrick Carnes, the national authority on sexual addiction, has written many books on the subject. Thanks to Dr. Carnes' work, we now understand the different levels of this addiction.

The biggest surprise in working with sex addicts was the discovery of sexual anorexia. Usually when we think of anorexia, we think about the eating disorder. Many people, therefore, think sexual anorexia means sexual starvation. In his book *Sexual Anorexia: Overcoming Sexual Self-Hatred*, Dr. Carnes defines the set of characteristics specific to sexual anorexia:

- Resistance to anything sexual

- Continued pattern of avoidance even to the detriment of a relationship

- Avoiding at all cost of sexual contact and attention

- Rigid and judgmental attitudes toward sexuality

- Resistance and avoidance of deeper, more painful issues

- Extreme shame and self-loathing about one's body, sexual attributes, and experiences

- Obsessing about sex and how to avoid it

- Possible episodes of sexual bingeing or periods of sexual compulsivity

I am amazed by the number of sexual anorexics—both women and men—in our culture. *Imprints of sexual anorexia are: Sex is dirty, sex is a sin, sex is shameful, sex is abuse, sex is pain; withholding sex is power and self-protection. The most harmful imprints are: I am bad, I am unworthy, I don't deserve God's love.*

Whatever the imprint, the sexual anorexic's primary goal is to find ways not to combine intimacy with sex. Most sexual anorexics are silent about it and rarely get diagnosed; when they do come to treatment, it is not for sexual addiction, but for divorce issues or depression.

Unfortunately, Sexual Anorexia is only one level of the addiction. Sexual addiction is also associated with risk-taking and high-risk behaviors affecting all areas of the sex addict's life. For some sex addicts, that will mean illegal activities such as exhibitionism, making obscene phone calls, or molestation. However, the majority of sex addicts do not necessarily become sex offenders.

Behaviors associated with sexual addiction include:

- Compulsive masturbation
- Multiple affairs (extra-marital)
- Multiple or anonymous sexual partners and/or one-night stands
- Consistent use of pornography
- Unsafe sex
- Phone or computer sex (cyber-sex)
- Prostitution or use of prostitutes
- Exhibitionism
- Obsessive dating through personal ads
- Voyeurism (watching others) and/or stalking
- Sexual harassment
- Molestation/Rape
- Sado/Masochism or violent sex
- Bestiality

In all of the above scenarios, sex is a drug; it is a medicator for deeper issues and imprints.

When Billy came to us, he was angry and confused. He had just been confronted at work about his sexual behavior, resulting in the loss of a high-powered position. He was a great and talented professional. He could not understand how his superiors could fire him because he had had an affair; after all, he figured, everyone does it. This position was the third one Billy had lost due to inappropriate sexual conduct and affairs. Once again, he had risked losing everything because of his addiction, but Billy could not see that. This time around, he even lost his marriage and his child. Yet he rationalized his behavior. As we started working on his imprints and the suppressed pain motivating his behaviors, we discovered that Billy had been sexually abused and terrorized in his childhood. His father had sexually abused Billy's sister while Billy was forced to watch without being able to rescue her. If he cried and tried to stop his father, he would get a beating followed by being masturbated. Billy's imprints were the blueprint for his sexual acting out. *His imprints were: Sex is fear, shame, pain, violence; it is hidden and dangerous. Men are overpowering, abusive and violent. I have no right to sexual boundaries. A man can break those boundaries. I am weak and bad because I could not save my sister so I don't deserve love and happiness. I am a man so I can do what I want.* All of Billy's imprints were mixed with sexual arousal and pleasure. Billy had no sexual boundaries, and for him, sexual activity was related to danger, pain, and a profound feeling of unworthiness that translated into self-sabotage. With time, he recovered, totally changed his life, and regained his sanity and dignity. Now he's happily married and has a brand new career.

Another of our clients, Brian, had discovered his father's pornographic magazines when he was eight years old. He used to look at them secretly and be aroused. His older brother showed him how to masturbate. The porno images were connected to self-gratification. At thirty-eight, Brian had a wife, two children, and a successful business. Unfortunately, Brian was addicted to pornography, cyber-sex, and masturbation. After a failed attempt at treatment and recovery, he lost his marriage and then neglected his business to the point of bankruptcy. *His imprint was: Sex is self-gratification and visual stimulation. Intimacy is for sissies. Love is working and providing for family. I am entitled to my pleasure and gratification.*

Julia was a beautiful woman with the body of a model. She was narcissistic, and her greatest pleasure was sexually seducing and enticing men. Her body and her sexuality were her power. Because she grew up in a poor family, she promised herself not to be poor when she was an adult. Her body and her beauty were her ticket out of poverty. Men showered her with gifts and money. She did not find pleasure in the sexual act but from how her being desired gave her power over men. *Julia's imprint was: Being rich is having power. Being beautiful and desired is being rich. Without beauty and youth, there is no value.* When she turned fifty, Julia had numerous plastic surgeries and spent a fortune trying to look twenty. She was alone and eventually had a meltdown, which got her into therapy; her therapist referred her to us. At Pavillon, Julia discovered her Identity and her Inner Beauty. She discovered her true calling, went back to school, and became a certified Life Coach specializing in women's issues.

Judy came to us in bad physical shape. She started cutting herself and using the drug Ecstasy when she was sixteen. Images in the media convinced her that she was not thin enough and she needed to belong to the "In" crowd of thin girls in order for the boys to notice her. Although Judy was 5'6" and weighed 102 lbs, she saw herself as heavy. Slowly, Judy started understanding the imprints she has received regarding her body. She had bought into the media standards of beauty since she was a little girl. Her father and brother had magnified this imprint by their comments about pretty thin women. Judy managed to change her imprints as well as her behavior. She graduated from college with a degree in journalism.

The mass media today has come to have a powerful influence on the imprints we create. Why? Have you ever noticed that the mass media's members have not been elected as "officials" by anyone; they are not accountable to anyone, yet they shape the standards, the rules, and morals for the majority of people.

One of society's collective imprints is a dependence on "authorities." In the twenty-first century, we have turned the media and Internet into a social authority. They tell us what we need to do, how we need to look and dress, and what cars we need to drive. They tell us what's in and out. The media tell us which illness is going to get us and which pill will make us happy. They determine how we should vote, think, and feel. Mostly, they influence whom we should fear and hate.

For centuries, we were programmed into believing that religious and/or state authorities had the truth, knowledge, power, and wisdom to save us, help us, and take care of us, but that protection and assistance was always contingent on our obedience and adherence to their rules and dogmas. As a society, our values came via the opinions, evaluations, and rules perceived authorities set for us. They had the power to decide whether we were good or bad. "They" had the control over our codependent minds. Our hierarchical systems fostered that dependence which basically said:

- *Our values, our happiness, and our success come from others and from outside of ourselves.*

- *Others are responsible for our happiness*

In that belief system and imprint, things are done to us or withheld from us, and we are victims at the mercy of the system without a way out. Our own beliefs and perceptions keep us stuck in the prison of our minds.

To paraphrase one of my mentors, Rev. Michael Beckwith, in the twenty-first century, the mass media has become the ultimate weapon of "mass distraction." From the overload of information given to us, our minds have begun to reject this constant bombardment, and we are now starting to wake up to the higher dimension of our lives and our minds.

Imprints are like skeletons in the closets of our minds. They are there, but no one knows it. In the early years of child development, we are like sponges; we take in the messages at a great speed. Unfortunately, we do not have the maturity and necessary discernment to distinguish between true and false.

In some of our programs, we would have entire families in attendance at the same time. What was interesting was that we could have five children or more from the same family, yet each one would have a different perception of the family dynamics, and a lot of their imprints would differ, yet the basic ones would prevail.

As a species, we still run on our reptile/primitive brain coding and imprint of "fight or flight"—our fear- and anger-motivated behaviors. The cultures of entire nations are still anchored in those imprints.

The good news is that positive imprints are also internalized during this early period of childhood development. It is much easier to get in touch with positive imprints after we have removed the influence and pain of the negative ones. Now that we understand about negative imprints, let's turn to some positive imprints we can use to replace them.

10   Light at the End of the Tunnel

As is the case with negative imprints, positive imprints also form and shape our values, our strengths, and our characters. They are the silver lining. They are the hidden treasure, hidden because the pain and dysfunction brought by negative imprints overshadows them. Nevertheless, they are the positive and creative side of us; they are very much part of our Authentic Self and of our intellectual, emotional, and spiritual make-up.

I have received some great treasures from my parents and will only name a few of the many here as examples.

Positive Imprints from My Mother:

Creativity	Her basic belief was that you can create beauty out of anything. Whatever she touched—clothing, knitting, cooking, dressing, writing—all had a very personal and creative touch. I have internalized that to the point of making it a profession, first in liturgical arts and later in re-sculpting and re-shaping human lives. *My imprint: Creativity is essential; it is beauty expressed; it is the sweetness of life. It is powerful communication.*
Resourcefulness	Mom could find a way no matter what. She could make something out of nothing. She was a great researcher and would find solutions. If you lost something, Mom had an extra sense for finding it. I have inherited her resourcefulness. *My imprint: Contained within the problem is the solution; with patience and perseverance you'll find it*

Arts and Culture:	I was six years old when mom took me to my first museum, and I was eight when she took me to my first opera, *Madame Butterfly*. Mom explained the story to me, and we both cried. I saw beauty and art, as well as the richness of the culture through my mother's eyes. She taught me to feel beauty and respect it. She gave me my love of learning. Mom had a mystic quality about her, and she knew how to focus on the essential. I will be forever grateful to have the same. *My imprint: Art and culture are the essence of my sensitivity, passion, and ability to marvel*
Being A Graceful Hostess:	In time of war, lack of food and ingredients, with the little we had, Mom used to make meals look like feasts. She knew how to cut a cookie into many delicate pieces and put some flowers on the plate so it looked abundant and delicious. She would invent exotic names for her dishes. In 1943, all we had was Army-issued cornbread as hard as a brick. Mom would make pretty slices, then soak them in hot water and garnish the slices with little pieces of apples; she would call them Olga's wonder sticks. To this day, I love being a hostess and serving my guests the way she did. *My imprint: People are special; serve them in such a way that they will remember being special in your presence.*
Civic and Social Involvement:	My mother was an activist. She was politically conscious with a great sense of justice, fairness, and civil rights. The war went against all of her beliefs. She took risks in order to speak up, especially after the war. She stood up for the poor and the underprivileged. She had a heart of gold. She was a great volunteer. I have internalized my mother's social causes and civil duty, political awareness, and fairness. I have been a generous, responsible, engaged contributor in all the societies where I have lived. *My imprint: Service and volunteering are a privilege, honor, and responsibility.*

In another book, I plan to pay special tribute to my step-mom. She's ninety-one and a true treasure. Nana is the living proof that we can change and transform at any age.

Positive Imprints From My Father:

Love Of Travel And Adventure:	My dad loved to travel, to discover, to learn about and get to know other cultures. He changed countries and continents looking for a better life. He did not have a good sense of direction so we would frequently get lost, but it never prevented us from getting where we were going. He had a childlike joy in the process of discovering. My love of travel, adventure, and discovery come straight from my dad. *My imprint: Let's go! There's one more wonderful place to discover. I will find my way no matter what.*
Risk Taking:	Throughout his life, in order to survive, Dad took some major risks. Escaping from the Russian front, leaving Croatia for Paris with $40 in his shoe, immigrating to Canada, and finally, spending his last years with us in North Carolina are but a few of the major risks he took. He changed jobs in order to provide for us. I have internalized my Father's spirit of courage and risk-taking as well as his ability to adapt to change to survive. *My imprint: We can overcome this. It is better to risk and fail than not to do it at all.*
Love Of Music:	No matter how tough life was, my dad loved to sing. I remember as a little girl, during the war, when I was afraid but had to walk in the dark, I would sing a song to give myself courage. Dad loved to dance and so do I. *My imprint: Music is Joy and Love. It chases the fear and sadness away. Dancing makes the body happy!*
Love Of Nature:	Dad possessed a childlike enthusiasm for Nature and animals. He loved being in the woods; he loved skiing. He loved the Adriatic Sea; he loved oceans. He was a great diver; he would dive for shells. He taught me how to swim, and he taught me reverence for Nature and to love animals. He taught me how to preserve Nature and how to befriend animals. He had a great sense of timing and patience with them. He tamed a squirrel who would come to eat out of his hand. *My imprint: Animals are our friends. They love us unconditionally. We are responsible for our environment.*

Great Work Ethic:	My dad was a hardworking man, a responsible, devoted, and loyal employee. He was punctual. He walked the extra mile. He was a team player. He was extremely grateful for the opportunity to earn a living. He loved his jobs, and he was well-loved by all of his employers. I have fully inherited my father's work ethic and have been a devoted and loyal employee as well as employer. *My imprint: A productive day is a productive life. The joy of a job well done and the gratitude in your heart will guarantee a good night's sleep.*
Fiscal And Civil Responsibility:	My father taught me the value of democracy, the importance of voting, and the love of freedom. He instilled in me the honor of fiscal responsibility. He was so proud when we became Canadian citizens, and he did not miss a single election; he proudly cast his vote. He would have been so proud of my husband and me, when we became U.S. citizens. That was one of his dreams. *My imprint: Honesty, Loyalty, Integrity, and Democracy are the true freedoms.*

As you can see, I assimilated a lot of good, regardless of the negative imprints. When we become aware and we consciously understand our lives, only then do our lives have worth. I am so grateful I was part of my family and shaped and molded both by life and by these two sweet spirits.

As a young student in Paris, my imprints were also greatly influenced by my art teacher. His teaching had a magical quality. He was a wonderful storyteller who made each artist come alive as he told their individual stories, how they thought, and what they wished to express in their artwork. My favorite story was about how Michelangelo created the statue of David. First, he chose a very odd shaped piece of marble. When the other artists asked him what he was going to do with such an odd shape, he replied that he was going to bring David out of it and into life.

Years later, my husband and I had a chance to visit Florence and the *Galleria dell'Accademia*, the home to the statue of David. In Florence, there are a few different statues of David, all by great artists. However, there is only one *David*.

When you enter the Galleria, there is silence and anticipation. Everyone can feel that something special is about to happen...and then, there it is. David, standing in all his magnificence. The primary difference between other statues of David and Michelangelo's David is that the other artists captured David as the King of Israel; only Michelangelo captured David's spiritual mission and essence. Michelangelo chiseled and chiseled until he revealed the true David.

Similarly, our imprints and the pain in our lives are the necessary marble out of which emerges our true essence as well as our spiritual mission. Little did I know when I was still an art student that someday I would find my true essence by taking the road less traveled, the path to recovery, and that my inner journey would lead to transformation and freedom.

My childhood religious experience of God was painful and confusing. The enmeshment of church and politics of that time augmented the confusion. Many times I heard that people were made in God's image and likeness. This statement perpetuated my childhood image of a judge on a throne in great need of anger-management classes. I could not equate God with Love.

My imprints kept me from understanding the concept that we were made in God's image. In my belief system, as I experienced bad things being done to me, the major question I asked through a good portion of my life was, "*Why me?* Why are you doing this to me?" At that time, I believed in the power of "them" and "they," and I lived at the mercy of external forces and events.

Through pain and my inner journey, through a near-death experience, recovery, and love, I have discovered my very own essence and oneness with God. I have discovered my spiritual mission as well as my Divine Imprint.

Thom Rutledge, a psychotherapist, speaker, and author, in his article, "Don't Start a War Just Because You Don't Feel at Peace" describes so well the two E's of my era—Extremism and Exclusivity—which are still prevalent today:

> It is about fundamentalism. And you can be a fundamentalist anything—fundamentalist Christian or Muslim, fundamentalist atheist, fundamentalist republican or democrat, fundamentalist boy scout, whatever. I have a friend who is a fundamentalist hippie.
>
> Living according to the philosophy of "Close Your Mind and Open Your Mouth," will bring us nothing but more grief, heartache and hardship.

I totally agree with Mr. Rutledge. He also says, "Listen with your ears not your fears." At that time in my life, everything was heard through fear, and consequently reacted to, out of my ego.

I had no understanding at the time that my role on this planet is to be a co-creator. At that time, I did not know that we are energy. I did not know that within me is the wisdom and the power to transform, nor did I know that I was called to co-create a brand new life. I was living in the belief system that *I will believe it when I see it*. I had no clue that life requires the opposite: *I can only see it if I believe it*.

11 Co-Creation

Understanding my Divine Imprint now brings me to the principles of co-creation. The shift in our self-perception is the point where we stop being a victim and become a co-creator with God, with life, and the universe. Let me illustrate by describing a true transformational and co-creative process—the metamorphosis of a butterfly.

Nori Huddle did extensive scientific research on the metamorphosis of a caterpillar into a butterfly. It is an amazing process we can relate to our own spiritual transformations as we move from our negative imprints to understanding our Divine Imprint.

The caterpillar, stuck in his caterpillar encoding, certainly cannot envision himself flying. Yet impulsively, the caterpillar forms the chrysalis to start the transformation process. Within the chrysalis are the caterpillar's new cells called "imaginal cells." These cells contain the genetic coding of the butterfly. They are so totally different from the caterpillar cells that the caterpillar's immune system gobbles them up, seeing them as foreign.

The imaginal cells continue to multiply, holding within them the perfect pattern of the butterfly to be. They multiply at a great speed and overcome the immune system's attacks. Finally, the caterpillar seizes to struggle against the change, surrenders, and the imaginal cells take over.

The little tiny imaginal cells start to clump together into friendly little groups. They all resonate together at the same frequency, passing information from one to another.

And then the miracle of transformation occurs. Suddenly, these cells realize they are different from the caterpillar's cells; they discover and KNOW they are the cells of a butterfly. Now they are a multi-celled organism—a family of cells that can share the work and co-create the final stage of the butterfly's birth.

We are not different from the butterfly. Within each of us is the Divine genetic coding. Our Spiritual DNA contains the full pattern of who we are and what we came to be and do. Like the caterpillar, we have to surrender and die to the old ego ideas, beliefs, and imprints.

Ego wants to hang onto the smallness, the selfishness, the "control" and fears because it has no higher vision. Ego is the self-limiting vision, the caterpillar encoding in us. Ego operates out of our reptile brains and stimulates reptilian behaviors: obsessive-compulsive behaviors, dominance, aggression, submission, greed, jealousy, and competition. Ego is not Ungodly; it is *non*-godly, and at its core, it truly thinks it is God. When the prefrontal cortex is added to the animal brain, the intellect becomes the tool of the ego.

Ego has no ability to see our beauty and possibilities. Ego does not know that it is only the shadow of the Light we are. "We" are not the content of our minds. We are Transcendental Consciousness. Like the caterpillar's cells, our ego attacks our immune system and our physiology by feeding us the lies of our impossibilities and limitations, yet our imaginal cells, our Divine Imprint, and our impulse are stronger. A part in us knows deep down at our core that there is more to us; that our finest hour is yet to come.

Our Divine Imprint and our Spiritual DNA are much stronger than the Ego. Dr. Michael Beckwith, author of *Spiritual Liberation*, describes very eloquently the Divine Imprint by stating:

> The all wise, all-knowing something, we call God, has never performed a meaningless act. This means you are not an accident. God has a meaning for your life; God is the meaning. Your existence is born of Spiritual parentage. Your DNA is Divine Love, Divine Intelligence and Divine Creativity.

This meaning is what we came to express on this planet. Life's impulse is to be more, to expand, to express, and to grow. Whatever is not expressed ends up being depressed. Your destiny and mine is to be this Authentic and Creative Self. Like the caterpillar, we might forget this truth, we might believe we cannot fly, yet our Spiritual Identity knows the truth and has the ability to soar. The whole purpose of Spiritual work can be summed up as: Potentiality becomes Actuality.

Some of you reading these words may have the old imprint that God is simply a psychological crutch for the weak. I want you to know that I hear you, and I respect your imprint and perspective. After thirty-two years of working down in the trenches and witnessing transformations, I am like the doctors in trauma units who have witnessed miracles and become believers. I ask you to be patient with me to the end of this work. I believe we will meet and come to a mutual understanding by then.

We exist in a beautiful, orderly, organic, ever-evolving universe, governed by physical and spiritual laws. To experience fully the possibilities of this universe, I had to become aware that I was *energy*. I had to align my energy with these laws in order to experience synergy, synchronicity, harmony, love, and compassion.

"We do not create energy, we distribute it, and in the natural sciences we know that we transform energy from one type to another."
— *The Science Of Mind*

There are many expressions of energy:

Physical Energy:	Horsepower, athletic power, nuclear power, etc.
Sexual Energy:	Pure pro-creative energy
Mental/Intellectual Energy:	The Power of Thought and Mind Everything created is first a Vision and a thought. We live in a mental world first that then becomes material. Mental energy is creative energy. Science/causality etc.
Emotional Energy:	Emotions are the primary source of human energy, aspirations, and drive. They activate our innermost feelings; they contain our purpose in life and our values. Their key factor is the way we perceive and interpret circumstances. If viewed through our past experiences and belief system, (our imprints), we will respond *reactively* and automatically with an emotion that will be inappropriate and self-defeating. If viewed through our Identity/Authentic Self, we will respond *pro-actively*, creatively, responsibly, constructively, positively, and out of freedom of choice. Our Authentic Self is our Emotional Competency. It is the self found at our core. It is the part of us *not defined by our roles and possessions.* Our Authentic Self contains our talents, skills, unique gifts, interests, insights, passions, wisdom, and strengths. It is our genuine, self-authored, or endorsed self. It is a self that is aligned and congruent.
Spiritual Energy:	Contains the attributes of God within us: Beauty, Love, Freedom, Joy, Ecstasy, Bliss Spiritual Energy expresses our consciousness. Consciousness is one expression of the Infinite Field of Infinite Power.

Fig. 11-1: Expressions of Energy

I will talk about Spiritual Energy at greater length throughout the rest of this book. Our Spiritual Energy is what frees us from our negativity and what holds us back from being and doing what is intended for us.

When we access our Spiritual Energy, we vibrate at a higher frequency. Dr. David Hawkins, in his book *Power vs. Force: The Hidden Determinant of Human Behavior*, describes very well the hierarchy of levels of consciousness. His work is a real eye opener because it explores the different degrees of energy in relation to our emotions by using kinesiology to calibrate energy frequencies.

Hawkins describes shame as the lowest frequency (the one that is close to death and suicide) calibrating at the frequency of 20. Courage calibrates at 200, Love at 500, and Enlightenment is the highest Frequency calibrating at 700 to 1,000, which is pure consciousness.

Freud, Einstein, and Newton calibrate at 499 because they were religious. They did not make it to level 500 (Unconditional Love). At level 500, we transcend religion (dependence) and get to Spirituality (Co-creation) and the Self unfolds. You touch the heart and vibrate at the frequency of Compassion and Reverence.

When we are in our Authentic Self and we are tapping into our Divine encoding, we vibrate and calibrate at a much higher frequency of Spiritual Energy which is Love. This higher vibration can only happen when we are in touch with our heart and when we align our Emotional and Spiritual Energy with our actions.

12 Accessing the Authentic Self:
First Action Steps to Transformation

To access the Divine Imprint and our imaginal cells, in other words our Authentic Self, like the caterpillar, we must undergo the process of emotional transformation. We need to take the necessary steps to access the beauty, the greatness, and the uniqueness within us. We need to take the Inner Journey. We do so by embracing a transformational process and by taking action.

The Core Action Steps to Transformation

1. **Awareness**—Becoming Aware
2. **Admittance**—Admitting our point of departure
3. **Release**—Releasing and letting go of "it"
4. **Willingness**—Becoming willing to change, and allowing change to happen
5. **Forgiveness**—Radical Forgiveness

As a result of the above actions we will experience:

- A shift in self-perception
- Revelations will follow

We then need to continue the process of transformations and take more action steps:

6. **Gratitude**—Practice daily the attitude to gratitude
7. **Meditation**—Visualization and Affirmations
8. **Building** and Maintaining Consciousness
9. **Acceptance of Love**—Love is the Way

The First Action Step To Transformation: Awareness

> "Until you make the unconscious conscious, it will direct your life and you will call it fate."
>
> —Carl Jung

We need to become aware. As Carl Jung said, we need to become conscious of the unconscious. *Webster's Dictionary* defines being aware as "having knowledge, being conscious and informed" and the antonym provided is "oblivious." I have spent a good portion of my life oblivious to my Inner Reality and Truth, and I have worked with thousands of clients who were equally oblivious.

To choose to be conscious of the unconscious, we must become aware of our Inner state, beyond our roles and possessions. To do so, we must ask ourselves the following questions and be honest in writing our responses.

How safe are the streets of my mind for others and myself to walk on?

Which of our imprints, deep-seated beliefs, and perceptions govern our lives? Which are the imprints we have internalized and still believe? We may know differently with our intellect, but what do our guts say and believe? What dramas are we displaying in our lives?

- What do we truly believe about ourselves, others, life, God, death, money, marriage etc.?

- Who or what do we truly trust?

- What are our values?

- What are our priorities in life?

- Who are we?

- How do we behave?

- Why do we do what we do?

- Who is responsible for our life, our happiness, our misery?

- What are we afraid of?

- Are we still victims of circumstances and others?

- Do we still feel that "they" are doing it to us?

Where do we stand with our self-esteem? (Self-esteem is based on self-respect—we can't expect others to respect us if we do not respect ourselves. It is self-care. Self-respect is not about what we do, but who we are. It is about feeling valued. It's about loving ourselves just because we are. Self-respect is the cornerstone on which many other attributes are built such as honesty, confidence, and integrity. Our sense of value and respect starts in childhood. It is through the love of our parents and environment and by getting our basic needs met that we first come in contact with our sense of self-value. On our way toward our Authentic Self, reviewing our definition of respect will direct us toward those areas that need attention.)

- What defines us?
- Where do we stand with our self-worth?
- What are our intentions and the driving forces in our lives?
- What is our motivation in life?
- Do we feel we are good enough, valuable enough, loved enough, important enough, etc.?
- What do we expect from ourselves in every area of our life?
- Do we measure up to our own expectations?
- What do others expect from us? Do we feel we measure up to their expectations?
- What do we expect of others? Do they measure up to our expectations?
- Do we have enough time, money, success, accomplishments, and love, or do we have feelings of lack and limitation?

We need to ask ourselves these basic questions in order to be aware of what goes on inside of us. Ego has a tendency to numb our feelings and make us go through life and daily events in a mechanical, automatic way. Some of us try to "fit" in and be like everyone else; some of us rebel and go the other way. We become human doings unaware of the incredible potential within us. We need to become aware of these barriers so we can move beyond them.

> "Your task is not to seek love, but merely to seek and find all the barriers within yourself that you have built against it."
> —Rumi, 13th century mystic poet

The Second Action Step To Transformation: Admittance

I need to admit the truth to myself. *Truth Sets Me Free!*

- What is our truth?
- What is our story? What are we saying to others about ourselves?
- What is our inner talk? What is our inner critic saying?
- What are the voices of our inner committee saying?
- What are the value systems directing our life?

In his tapes *Revolution of Values*, Dr. Beckwith challenges us to take a closer look at where we are internally and what do we really value.

Are we stuck in the Natural Value System: an eye for an eye—a tooth for a tooth? This value system brings *survival, aggression, and conquest.* The predominant fear of this value system is fear of dying. It makes us feel separate and alone, addicted to power and control.

Are we operating from the Hedonistic Value System: This is the "Let's Feel Good" system, with its predominant fear of pain. This value system has turned us into an instant gratification society and made us addicted to sensations. Unpleasant feelings and pain must be numbed with medicators or heightened with high-risk behaviors.

Are we focused in the Materialistic Value System: *accumulation, greed, scarcity, lack of ethics, the "not enough" syndrome,* which keeps us in Security Addiction with its predominant fear—Fear of Loss.

Are we stuck in the Humanistic Value System: The need to be popular, well liked, important, to be number one! This value system fosters codependency. The greatest need in this system is to belong and the predominant fear is Fear of Abandonment bringing with it the Addiction to Suffering as well as the Addiction to Power and Control. This system's main characteristic is chronic Perfectionism.

Are we operating from the Religious Value System: We must do the right thing to gain favor from God. This system operates on the premise that God is a mean judge withholding our good, and punishing or rewarding us. The predominant fear is: Fear of Punishment and Hell. Main characteristics of this system are self-righteousness, fanatic beliefs, guilt, feelings of separation, not measuring-up to expectations of perfectionism, rigidity, and exclusivity. This system triggers all Core Addictions as well as dependencies and Codependence with its people-pleasing, caretaking, martyrdom, and chronic perfectionism. This system also fosters extremism.

Finally, are we operating from the Spiritual Value System: based on the Principle of Oneness and Beingness. It is based on the Law and Principle of Growth and Inner Values. Predominant strengths of this system are: inner wisdom, courage, trust, understanding, and love. The predominant characteristics of this system are: humility, openness, flexibility, inclusiveness, forgiveness, compassion, and connectedness.

"Don't be just good...be good for something"

Henry David Thoreau

- Whatever we value becomes the quality of our consciousness!
- Whatever we dwell on becomes our reality!
- Whatever we keep on denying, keeps running our lives!

This second action step requires us to admit to ourselves where we stand so we can change. As we change our imprints, our thinking, our feelings, and our behaviors, our lives transform. As the butterfly realizes how different it is from the caterpillar, so we realize we are not human beings trying to have a spiritual experience, but we are Spiritual Beings, having many human experiences. Our entire self-perception is now shifting.

We also need to admit to ourselves the kind of relationship we have with our Creator. Is it a "call 911" type of relationship? Do we call on God only when we are in trouble and want an emergency saving? A friend of mine used to describe his Power/Control Addiction as "Okay, God; now that I am up and awake, you can go to sleep; I'll take care of everything"; in other words our egos continue running our lives until the next crisis when we need emergency saving.

Do we plead, bargain, or make false promises with this invisible Power? Do we simply dismiss It as the crutch for the weak and deny Its existence? Or do we trust this Presence and Power within us, around us, through us, as us?

How many false gods do we have? Through a big portion of my life, as well as the lives of many people I know, the true powers in life were the power of money, sex, and relationships, and the power of all the other medicators. These powers were trusted in place of the Power of God. They were the false Gods. I know many people who can talk about God very eloquently but do not trust God. It is not about talking the talk; it is about walking the walk.

TRUTH SETS US FREE. Admitting our point of departure facilitates our desired point of arrival.

The more honest we are with ourselves, the faster we can get out of our Ego's lies, rationalizations, justifications, and excuses. When we embark on a transformative path, second force kicks in and Ego starts to rationalize. Remember, our imaginal cells and our Spiritual encoding are by far more powerful than the best of the Ego's lies.

Our Soul knows. Our Identity, our Authentic Self wants freedom and self-expression. This is no time to quit. This is the time for self-respect and self-care. We are on our way to a New Self and a new life.

The Third Action Step To Transformation: Release—Letting Go Of "It"

This action step requires us to let go of all the negativity that stands in our way. Our negative imprints and negative beliefs are a drain of energy. Shame, guilt, and grief keep our energy calibrating under 100. *Webster's Dictionary* defines release as: "to free from confinement and bondage and to surrender."

Release means to set our Authentic Self free from the confinement and bondage of our imprints and ego. My old imprint was: *Never surrender; you must resist and fight or you will lose control. If you lose control "they" will take advantage of you.* The ridicule of this imprint is that I never had the control.

So what is surrender?

- To realize the futility of repeating the same patterns and expecting different results.

- To realize the pain and struggle caused by trying to control outcomes.

- Being in the present, the now moment, versus past or future.

- The willingness to let go of outcomes.

- The willingness to change and do the work.

- The realization that we don't know, we don't have the answers, and we need help.

- The willingness and humility to experience our own intellectual or emotional vulnerability in order to experience our spiritual strength and the strength of our character.

- Embracing our Authentic-Self, our Inner Excellence.

- Paradoxical thinking/feeling: Our negative imprints, perceptions, feelings, attitudes, and behaviors are automatic and they disempower our Authentic Self. As we admit our powerlessness over them, we become *empowered*. We experience a Paradigm Shift. A shift in our belief system: our fear and mistrust level are lowered and replaced with hope and trust.

"By holding on, we destroy what we hope to preserve; by letting go, we feel secure in accepting what is."

—Margaret Wheatley

The 4th Action Step To Transformation: Willingness And Permission To Change

Mary's imprint was: *Don't rock the boat. Do not change anything. Change is scary.* The hidden message of this imprint was: *Denial is the way to deal with unpleasant reality.* This imprint keeps in place the unspoken rules and dysfunctional patterns. It does not leave room for considering possibilities, for thinking outside the box, but leaves us stagnant.

This action step to Transformation requires us to be willing to change. It requires us to give ourselves the permission to grow and mature. Life requires a resounding Sacred "YES" from us. Our language and inner talk need to be changed. Life takes us at our word: If I believe I can't, my reality will reflect the truth of my belief. Life will present me the obstacles and impossibilities that will confirm my belief of "I can't."

My old imprint said: *I can't trust others; they always disappoint me.* Life and people kept validating this belief. At this point, our Intention needs to be set. *It all begins with Intention.* Intention is using the mind for a higher purpose; it is bypassing the Ego's limited patterns of thinking as well as the Ego's habitual outcomes and procedures.

When we establish a clear Intent and we hold that Intent in the magnetic field of our heart and our belief, we call forth actual Consciousness (awareness) of the universe and we tap into the Zero Point Field.

The Zero Point Field is an energy field in which all things come together. Some call it God; some call it an enormous energy field from which mankind can learn a great deal about life. It is the new frontier—the bridge where science and spirituality meet.

We experience the field every time we wrestle with a problem, trying to control its outcome and thereby not finding a solution. When sick and tired of struggling, we surrender and stop thinking about it; then, when we listen to our hearts and unthink the rational, the solution appears quickly and easily. We have all experienced that.

We need to be clear about our intent. If my intent is to be happy rather than to be right, that intent and choice will produce peace, harmony, happiness, and unity.

In this step, we need to fall in love with wellness and be willing to give up our pain and misery. Anger, hatred, willfulness, and control will poison our biology and our immune system. Love, gratitude, beauty, and joy will regenerate, rejuvenate, and heal our bodies and our entire biology.

This step requires our permission to step outside the web of drama and suffering that was created by our imprints, and instead, willingly and trustingly to lean into life. This step is one of courage and willingness to BE. This step is one of alignment of our energetic bodies, thereby allowing us to enter into the flow of life.

As any alpine/downhill skier knows, the Law of Gravity requires us to lean forward into the slope, rather than obey the body's impulse to lean backwards and resist the forward movement. The Law of Growth and self-actualization requires us to lean forward into our Authentic Self and give it our willingness, our attention, and our permission to unfold and come forth. As Nike's most successful ad says, "JUST DO IT!"

> *Today, I unlock my wild imagination and let it dance freely in a universe ready to reveal the threads of truth.*

The 5th Action Step to Transformation: Forgiveness—Radical Forgiveness

> "Hatred ever kills; love never dies. such is the vast difference between the two. what is obtained by love is retained for all time. what is obtained by hatred proves a burden in reality for it increases hatred."
> —Mohandas K. Gandhi

Why "radical" forgiveness? Resentment (especially justified resentments), blame, anger, and hate are toxic; they poison our entire biology. The absurdity of this dynamic is that the resentments I feel are like the cup of poison I am drinking, but I expect the resented person to die from it. It cannot happen. Resentments are like slow motion suicide; they are killing us and keeping us in the cycle of being victims or victimizers.

As Yoda said to Luke Skywalker in *Star Wars*, "No. Try not. Do, or do not. There is no try." To forgive does not mean we agree with the crime or transgression; to forgive is to reclaim one's power and Inner Authority. To forgive is an act of self-love. As I said in Step Four, life requires our permission to unfold. It requires our resounding "Yes" to our greatness and oneness.

Through my clinical work, many times I have seen addicts hanging on to their guilt and shame as a green light to relapse or act-out. They knew that if they truly forgave themselves the need to use would be removed, but they feared that freedom because it was unfamiliar.

Sharon's imprint was: *Others have the power to take my good from me. Others are dishonest and will take my money away.* She had been associated with her husband in a successful business. To expand the business, they took on another partner. A few years later, her husband divorced her. At this very vulnerable moment in Sharon's life, the other partner took fiscal advantage of her. In the process, Sharon was deprived of millions of dollars. Her worst fear had come to pass and her resentment was justified. She carried that resentment for a number of years, unable to forgive both men. It took a diagnosis of cancer for Sharon to wake up and push herself into Inner work. The result for her was forgiveness and self-empowerment. Now Sharon is happily re-married and is running a successful business.

Brian said to me, "It was much easier for me to forgive others than it was to forgive myself. My guilt kept me a little longer in the victim mode. I could suffer a little more! The status of being so bad attracted a lot of sympathy from others; it was my false value."

When we forgive ourselves, the question, "Why is this happening to me?" disappears. Instead, we become a channel, a conduit, and an instrument for greater good. Suddenly, we start having a connection and an inner sense of belonging. Rather than things happening to us, they start happening through us! We definitely operate at a much higher frequency. Dr. Hawkins calibrates acceptance/forgiveness at 350. Our entire biology reflects this energy flow.

Taking the steps of forgiveness we need to:

- Confront our emotional pain, shock, fear, anger, and grief.

- Recognize that the hurt has occurred; it may have been totally unfair, and these steps are not meant to minimize the hurt.

- Realize that forgiveness can occur only after we have processed our fear, anger, and grief.

- Understand that *love* is *what we ultimately want for ourselves* and *from ourselves*, and that forgiveness is a gift we are giving ourselves by reclaiming our Power and Inner Authority.

- Understand that forgiveness does not condone, approve, or forget the harmful acts.

- Realize that we are the only person capable of, and responsible for, our own feelings and for healing the hurt that is going on inside of us. Forgiveness is our key to freedom and peace.

Forgiveness can happen only in the "Now" moment, and when it does, it cancels the past and prepares a better future.

> The best thing is not to hate anyone, only to love. That is the only way out of it. As soon as you have forgiven those you hate, you have gotten rid of them. Then you have no reason to hate them; you just forget."
> —Hazrat Inayat Khan, founder of the Sufi movement

First Result and Benefit of Actions Taken: The Shift in Self-Perception

Having taken the previous action steps, we start experiencing the results and benefits. We take ownership of our Authentic Self. We have internalized a new belief: Just as a drop of the ocean contains all the ingredients of the entire ocean, we contain within us the qualities of our Creator.

By now, we understand that we are not simply children of God but rather an individualized expression of God/Creator/Light/Energy/Field. Give it the name you need and want—it does not matter. We are Co-Creators with this One. At this stage, we know we are channels, conduits, and instruments for our Creator to express, create, heal, and work through us and all around us. The Spiritual Awakening is happening. We start having a deep sense of belonging and the ability to connect to the Universal Wisdom that surrounds us.

Our vision and understanding of our Authentic Self is getting clearer at this point. We are regaining our Freedom of Choice.

Our perception is shifting from a world of lack, limitation, and not enoughness into a world where we are starting to see possibilities, a world of Abundance and Plenitude. Yes, we are starting to believe in a world that works for all. The new beliefs are gaining ground. Our imaginal cells are multiplying and our transformation is on the way.

> We have the power and the responsibility to choose and change our perceptions and beliefs... it is done to us according to our "BS" = belief system!

We make a list of our new beliefs; we give ourselves permission to have these beliefs without the need to be approved by anyone. We do not have the need to impose our beliefs on anyone. We honor our new beliefs and give them our sacred YES. We acknowledge the power our new beliefs have in transforming our lives.

Our Sacred "YES" empowers our freedom and brings us closer to the self-actualization of our Authentic Self.

Ann Marie belonged to a traditional organized religion that was fear-based. *Her imprint said: you must believe only like we do or you will burn in Hell.* Ann Marie's belief system held her a prisoner of Fear. Her greatest discovery came when she realized that Fear is absence of Love. It is the belief in separation from our Creator. Perfect Love casts away all Fear. Ann Marie called me, crying in joy, and said, "Liliane, I am free to believe in LOVE. Only Love is God, and I am Love." She has integrated this new belief system and it has empowered her truth.

We all have our truth. This step helps us discover it!

Second Result and Benefit of Action Steps Taken: Revelation

As a result of action steps taken, we start to experience answers, understanding, a deeper awareness, and a heightened consciousness. Suddenly, we have ears to hear and eyes to see. The inner chatter of the ego and old self-talk have shut down or are not as loud. *Mary's imprint kept saying: I am so confused. I don't know what I am supposed to do. The hidden message in this imprint is: your doubt and confusion justify your inertia and procrastination.*

When we quiet down, breathe, contemplate, and meditate, revelations follow. When we listen and we make a conscious effort to trust, we make discoveries.

Breathing slowly, we enter the silence and safety of our hearts. We listen and make a conscious effort to trust the revelations and discoveries. Our truth and our path become clearer.

We realize we live in an orderly universe governed by spiritual and physical laws. We live in a Universe based on principles and truth. We can trust these principles and truths. They are truths because they do not change.

The Law of Gravity is a truth: No matter how good or advanced you are, if you fall from the twelfth floor, you are going to hit the ground.

The Law of Buoyancy is the power to float or rise in a fluid. In our consciousness, the Law of Buoyancy is the Elasticity of Spirit; it is our cheerfulness. When we are aligned with this law, we are not easily depressed.

The Law of Cause and Effect (Ego wants this one to apply only to others), says that we cannot plant strawberries and reap oranges. If we send out hatred, we do not receive love—we attract more hatred.

The Law of Love (Expansion and Contraction) is the most important law. In the *Book of Mirdad*, Mikhail Naimy says, "You live that you may learn to love. You love that you may learn to live. No other lesson is required of mankind."

All our suffering is a result of infringement of Universal Principles. This misalignment with the principles will block our creative energy. Our imaginal cells contain our full spiritual encoding, and despite the Ego's attacks, they will prevail.

The result is our ability to align our energy with Universal Principles and Laws to allow for our growth and transformation. Our potential is revealed. Our intuition is sharpened. We start trusting the loving Inner Voice. We begin to be aware of the greatness and beauty within us. We start practicing new emotional and spiritual skills. We start being obedient to our Inner Voice.

My old imprint was: Resist authorities; you don't have to obey; authorities are mean and unfair. Don't do discipline—that's not cool (actually, in my day it was not "groovy"). The Action Steps help us practice the newly acquired emotional skill of listening and the newly acquired spiritual skills of obedience, discipleship, and discipline.

For years, these skills set my Ego into negative reactions. So let us take a look at these skills and what they mean:

- **Obedience** is defined as compliance with what is required by authority. I used to be in conflict with and reacted against authority. Here, our emotional skill of listening is coupled with our spiritual skill of obedience to our Inner Authority, our Identity. We are starting to hear and trust the Inner Voice. We become, through our Inner Voice of Truth, our own authority to follow. We are guided to obey what we intuitively know is best for us.

- **Discipleship** is an active adherent of a movement or philosophy. My Identity, my Authentic Self is the Disciple of Love. I adhere to the philosophy that my life is worthy, that I am a beloved child of the Universe, and that my Identity is by far more creative and powerful than all the false gods. I adhere to the philosophy that my life has a purpose and it is mine to express it. I am a disciple of Love and Creativity.

- **Discipline** means the development of the faculties by instruction and exercise. It comes from the Latin word *disciplinaire*, which means in part "to educate." Unfortunately, our culture tends to associate this word with training via punishment. In its pure and spiritual sense, discipline is my willingness and openness to be faithful by practicing new spiritual skills and beliefs to replace old self-limiting imprints.

Therefore, a deep sense of what is true spirituality starts to be revealed. We begin experiencing spirituality as everything that is positive, constructive, freeing, and creative. Ego is the opposite: it is negative, destructive, restraining, and it kills creativity.

Here is where our head and our heart begin to connect. This connection is reflected in our ability to be flexible and unattached to outcomes. We feel safe and get along with others. The willfulness is being replaced by willingness; we start using our energy more effectively. We now trust our hearts as well as our emotional and spiritual intelligence.

Self-discipline and order mark this phase of development. At this point, our consciousness becomes more organized and receptive. Acceptance of self, life, and others occurs. Now a powerful shift happens. We awaken to the possibilities of living proactively. We embrace our role as Co-Creators with God/Energy/Zero Point Field, and our energy and enthusiasm have shifted.

Where before we were running against the wind, now we feel ourselves flowing through life, supported and guided.

We start accepting our role in the world. We start to see the big picture of our life more clearly. The action steps taken have provided us with the discipline and pro-activity needed fully to access our natural abilities, talents, and gifts. Our Higher Purpose is being revealed and becomes our driving force. We have learned how to shut off the inner chatter and instead listen to the wisdom of our heart and intuition.

I will never forget how excited Dan was to discover his Authenticity and the Spiritual being that he was. *Dan's imprint was: you earn money through hard work and the sweat of your brow.* For years he was in careers that had little meaning to him. As he was diligently taking these action steps and truly listening to his heart, Dan discovered his true calling and passion. He went back to school to become a brilliant neuroscientist. He stepped out of the business world and into the world of healing. Dan did not run away hating business; he was grateful for the experience it gave him. Dan simply stepped forward with Love for a higher Intent.

> "Deep pleasure, joy, and knowing secure my mind and delight my heart as daily revelations tell me who I really am. I maintain a clear, clean focus as I fully take in the beauties of nature and the intuitive insights that god has for me."
>
> —Margaret Stortz

13 Accessing the Authentic Self: Steps 6 through 9 to Transformation

The 6th Action Step To Transformation: Gratitude

Gratitude is an energizer. In this step, we understand the lessons we came to learn. We start to understand the greater vision and purpose of our lives. In this step, we start feeling the Divine Order, synchronicity, and synergy of events.

With this step, I came to understand that the worst aspects and events of my life were the beginning of my greatest good. Each painful event from my past had birthed a strength in me, had shaped and molded my uniqueness, and was a blessing in disguise.

In this step, I gained the ability to rewrite my own history and see the blessings. Gratitude opened a deep level of understanding. My old imprint: *"They have wronged me; they owe it to me; life owes me; I am entitled"* was forever replaced with a new understanding: *I am in the school called life to learn the lessons my soul needs for my Spiritual growth. People, events, and circumstances are all necessary. To qualify it as good or bad is again to believe in duality instead of oneness. I choose Oneness.*

Gratitude shifted my relationship with myself, with my environment, and with God. Now I no longer simply experienced God's energy flowing through me as a channel. Now I experienced this ENERGY as me. Forgiveness and gratitude gave me the ability to know and accept my mission as I was promised in my near-death experience.

Gratitude is humility in action with no space for Ego's self-centeredness and self-importance. As we begin to surrender, we start experiencing moments of exhilarating Oneness. The Attitude of Gratitude becomes the most potent attractor factor in our lives. We cannot be grateful and still feel victimized. Gratitude is Love in Action. We cannot be both cynical and grateful. Gratitude is the dissolvent of doubt, worry, cynicism, and self-pity.

What are we grateful for today? At this point, we write a complete list of our gratitude for every area of our lives. For the past thirty-two years, I have been writing daily my gratitude list. It doesn't matter whether the list is large or small.

You can't count your blessings and still be depressed. Here are some examples. As I said, every day I make a list which begins *I am grateful that*:

- I have hot, running water.

- I have enough food.

- I have enough money to pay my bills.

- I have a wonderful, caring husband.

- I have wonderful children.

- I live in the United States, the best country in the world.

- I can spend my time making a difference for other people.

- I can write this book to share my story and to help others.

- I have wonderful, supportive, and caring friends.

- I have a rich past full of events that have made me strong.

Gratitude is the catalyst for many transformations. Through the years, I have witnessed so many marvelous shifts in lives and careers because people took time to count their blessings, to be grateful for what they have, and to realize the abundance in their lives far outweighed any worries or sense of lack. Here are a few examples of people I have worked with who transformed themselves as a result of learning to practice gratitude:

- Suzanne was a CPA who decided to become a public speaker and workshop leader helping others to demystify their relationships with money.

- Roger was a corporate executive who decided to follow his calling and become a minister, start a church, write a book, and help hundreds to a better life.

- One of my dearest teachers gave up a lucrative drug-dealing business to become one of our nation's great thinkers and teachers.

- Jonathan is a well-known cardiologist who had a very successful clinic. Now Jonathan runs a clinic in Bosnia helping children and women who are victims of organized rape as part of ethnic cleansing and genocide. He is restoring human hearts by teaching forgiveness, dignity, and self-love. Recently, Jonathan said that none of his diplomas gave him an intensive course in compassion and caring like being in Bosnia. Jonathan is completely fulfilling his life's purpose.

"Today, I use my creative heart to convey my gratitude and appreciation, in wild and wonderful words, for all the expression of love on the planet of my life."

Marsha Lehman

The 7th Action Step To Transformation: Meditation—Visualization And Affirmation

This action step produces mastery of the ego. The previous self-blame, self-rejection, and self-loathing are replaced with a deep understanding and appreciation for who we are. We experience a deep compassion for our origin, for our lives, and for our lessons.

I remember so vividly holding myself in a long and loving embrace, truly understanding where I came from and how brave and wise my soul was to survive all I had experienced.

A Course in Miracles says: "All your past except its beauty is gone, and nothing is left but the blessing." How true that statement is in relation to this step.

This step also requires us to define our Vision of ourselves and of our lives. As Dr. Michael Beckwith says, "Each one of us has a unique pattern for evolving our spiritual passion and power as we co-create life with our Source."

Now it is up to us to tap into our Vision. To tap into it effectively, we need to quiet and lower the inner chatter of our minds. Practicing mindfulness and meditation can replace that chatter.

Meditation is not so mysterious. Neuroscientists have found that people who meditate shift their brain activity to different areas of the cortex; brain waves in the stress-prone right frontal cortex move to the calmer left frontal cortex. This mental shift decreases the negative effects of stress, mild depression, and anxiety. There is also less activity in the amygdala, where the brain processes fear.

Benefits of Meditation

- **Physical:** Through deep breathing—the backbone of any meditation practice—muscle fatigue and tension are reduced because of increased oxygen circulation to the brain.

- **Emotional:** Less irritability, reduction of "fight or flight" response, and more emotional manageability. Meditation gives us perspective when we are confronted with a crisis, thus making our lives more manageable.

- **Mental:** Better mental focus, concentration, and creativity. Less stress and anxiety. A greater peace of mind. Meditation seeks to bring harmful and counter-productive feelings/imprints to the surface, so we can process them in order to access our inner truth and bring clearer reality to our lives.

- **Spiritual:** Greater self-awareness, the feeling of being more "connected," and a greater sense of purpose. In addition, meditation helps us to resolve past issues caused by our negative imprints.

Many ways to meditate exist; one of the most researched and documented techniques is Transcendental Meditation (TM). But whether we choose TM, Zen Buddhist, or Contemplative Meditation does not matter. Many practices are available today. We need to experiment and find the most suitable one for us. I have been meditating for the past thirty-four years of my life. I have used TM meditation, music meditation, Kundalini Yoga, and Breath Work Meditation; they all work. Different times and events in my life required different approaches. Starting with TM is a great beginning. The whole point is that we need to start slowing down and changing our automatic stress responses. Meditation makes us mindful and present.

With this step, we also clean up our self-talk and start the empowering language of affirmations. We call forth the eternal genius with such powerful affirmations as:

> "I deserve and express the very best that God/Life wants to express through me. The Genius code within me is now activated. Divine, Universal Intelligence within me expresses easily, powerfully, and freely. My imaginal cells are releasing the Love that I am. Embraced by pure Spirit/Infinite Energy, I am supported in all that I Am and Do! This Creative Energy restores my body temple and renews my mind! I AM GRATITUDE. I AM PEACE. I AM LOVE. I AM!"

We start a visualization process through which we affirm who and what we want to be, and what we want to express, to do, and to have. Our subconscious mind believed our negative imprints were true, so we acted out of them. Now we are reversing the process.

Vision Boards

A Vision Board is a powerful tool to help us change imprints and false, self-limiting beliefs. We collect beautiful and appealing pictures of what we desire and we couple those with powerful affirmations. The pictures serve to help us in our visualization process because they appeal directly to the right side of the brain. Our right brains, our creative selves, cannot distinguish between an experience that is imagined and one that is real. Just as the right brain was unable to reject the negative imprints, it cannot reject as invalid, wrong, or untrue the positive images and feelings we offer it. By its very nature, the right brain is compelled, over time, to reproduce in outer reality everything it accepts as true in the secret workshop of our mind.

For the past thirty-three years of my life, everything that I am, that I do, and that I have, has been visualized, affirmed, believed, and manifested. From the sale of property to the success of our mission, it was applied and it produced great results. From the ideal vacation to the healing of painful relationships in my life, as well as recovery from illnesses, the method never failed. From fear to love, from self-rejection to self-love, it all was accomplished through this method.

Neuroplasticity of the brain is now a known scientific fact. It is the brain's ability to reorganize itself by forming new neural connections throughout life. Neuroplasticity allows the neurons (nerve cells) in the brain to compensate for injury, disease, and traumas, and to adjust their activity in response to new situations or to changes in their environment. Visualization and affirmations help us form new neural connections.

We can change the way we perceive. We can change the way we think. And when we change the way we feel, our inner and outer reality changes too. Forgiveness is the dissolvent of negativity, and Gratitude is the transformer of energy. Gratitude is the energy that increases the good and aligns us with Universal energy.

The Vision Board brings into focus the new elements we choose to project upon the screen of our creative imagination. Ask Olympians how they got their medals, and you will be told, "Practice and visualization." They see themselves doing it, feeling it, believing it, and becoming it. Anyone who has worked with biofeedback knows when you are hooked to the machine and visualizing skiing on the slope or racing on a track, your muscles will respond the same way as if you were truly doing it.

Our Vision Board must consists of pictures and words/affirmations that our Authentic Self selects to define more clearly what it truly *is* and what it truly *wants to achieve and express.*

Working with the Vision Board accelerates the empowerment of our imaginal cells so they can release our true self: Whole, Creative, Loving, Confident, Peaceful, Dynamic, and Powerful.

The Reverend Jack Boland has compiled the very best material on Vision Boards, visualization, and affirmations in the *Master Mind Journal*, available from Renaissance Unity (www.RenaissanceUnity.org). Using a Vision Board and Affirmations are part of Rev. Boland's Transforming System. Years ago, I had the privilege of participating in the making of the very first Transforming System and Master Mind Journal. Let me give you one personal example.

Following my first husband's death, I felt I was ready for a relationship after I had been living alone. At that time, I met Dr. Joseph Murphy who had formerly been a Jesuit priest, but who had left the Church to become a metaphysician. Dr. Murphy presented at a conference I attended. I was so impressed with what he had to say that I asked him to give me an affirmation to help me attract the "right" partner for me. Dr. Murphy gave me a wonderful affirmation: *Divine Intelligence in me attracts a man who is marriageable, loyal, faithful, and prosperous. He is God in action.* After Dr. Murphy gave me the affirmation, he told me, "Now go home and BE IT."

Somehow I did not hear the last part about *being it*. I was repeating the affirmation without anything happening. When I reported to Dr. Murphy that it was not working, he replied, in his infinite wisdom, "Madame, it cannot work. In one sentence you have affirmed seven times that it is not working. It is done unto you according to your belief. The affirmation required you to be it." WOW!

That was the day I truly saw the extent of my negative inner affirmations. Constantly, we either affirm the negative outcomes or the positive, desired outcomes. But more than that, Dr. Murphy helped me truly to understand the law of Mental Equivalent: *I first need to become what I desire to attract*. So, I became marriageable, loyal, faithful, and prosperous—as you know, not long after, Gilles came into my life. In short, a Vision Board and Affirmations help us change our perceptions, imprints, and beliefs, and therefore, our lives.

The 8th Action Step to Transformation: Building and Maintaining Consciousness

In the movie *The Karate Kid* (1984), the teacher tells the student, "Wax on, wax off," meaning practice, practice daily. This action step is where we practice who we have become; we manifest a new set of behaviors. What used to be impossible is now becoming possible.

Free from attachments, cravings, and must haves, we are gaining mastery. Our priorities and values have shifted and are stabilizing.

This step is where we will access our Divine Imprint contained within our imaginal cells. While we were in ego consciousness, our predominant addictive patterns were Security Addiction, Power/Control Addiction, Sensation Addiction, and Addiction to Suffering.

Each of these has within our Identity/Authentic Self a different imprint. The opposite of Security Addiction is the Imprint of Abundance. What is Abundance? Ego thinks of Abundance in terms of Financial Prosperity.

ABUNDANCE is a spiritual law and truth. In essence, true abundance is freedom. It is our fundamental wellbeing. It is experiencing a fulfillment that has nothing to do with, nor depends upon, exterior conditions. When we live our reality fully conscious, present, and whole, we live abundantly.

The quality of our attention, presence, and engagement in the "Now" moment is the genuine measure of abundance; thus, it is our greatest capital asset at any given time. Abundance reflects a basic faith in the goodness of life, in the energy that helps us through the darkest moments of our lives.

Abundance is being open and receptive to the wisdom of our desire and our Soul's calling. Abundance helps us to synchronize and synergize our energies with our higher good, therefore, allowing us to experience our good. Now we have experienced a paradigm shift. From the land of lack and not enough, we have moved into the land of Plenitude and Freedom. Now the glass is full or half-full, but not empty.

The Divine Imprint for Power/Control Addiction is Empowerment and Manageability. What is Empowerment? It is the process of increasing our capacity to make choices and to transform those choices. Empowerment is the process that allows us to gain the knowledge, skill set, and attitudes needed to cope proactively with an ever-changing world and circumstances.

More than that, empowerment is our conscious contact with our creator. It is this synergistic relationship that sustains our energies at high frequency and allows the synchronicity of events. The more personal, loving, and passionate is our conscious contact, the more supported, loved, and cared for we feel. The more we get ourselves out of the way, the faster we feel empowered and start experiencing the serendipity of life.

And what is manageability? It is the opposite of control. When we are trying to control outcomes, more often than not, our Ego energy is involved. Manageability is when we have surrendered and are in the flow.

Manageability is the state of being inspired, empowered, and guided. It is the relaxed, trusting state of mind where our head is connected to our heart, and we operate from an Inner Knowing and our authentic Inner Authority. The office supply company Staples has a terrific marketing button. When pushed it says, "That was easy!" Manageability is the state of mind that says, "That was easy."

For me, a time when I experienced manageability happened when my husband and I moved our entire organization from Canada to North Carolina. Throughout the process, I kept saying to myself, "Divine Order is now established in every area of my life. There is a Divine Plan for my life and that plan is now unfolding." And it definitely did; everything went as planned. Later, when we moved from North Carolina to Texas, a friend of ours sent us the Staples button, which kept us affirming, "That was easy!" In spite of my Ego's aversion to moving, my Identity was stronger, so yes, it was easy!

Sensation Addiction vs. Enjoyment

Enjoyment is the opposite imprint to Sensation Addiction. In order for you truly to appreciate what I mean by Enjoyment, let me first define Sensation Addiction. It is the addiction that medicates our feelings and alters our moods in an attempt to alter reality.

Characteristics of Sensation Addiction

This addiction can use many medicators such as:
- Work
- Sex/Relationships

- Shopping/Compulsive Spending
- Gambling
- Overeating or self-starvation
- Excessive exercising
- Speeding
- High-risk behaviors (unsafe sex etc.)
- Creating crises and dramas
- Substances and chemicals

Here are some beliefs and imprints that trigger this addiction:

- Pain must be immediately relieved or intensified
- Instant gratification of senses and appetites is necessary
- Instant solutions and cures are required
- Altering moods will alter reality
- Repeating the same patterns will produce different results
- Appearances are more important than character

Predominant Ego Feelings:

Passive:	Aggressive:
Bored	Invincible
Dissatisfied	Entitled
Anxious	Pressured...Over-Excited
Feeling Antsy	Obsessed
Impatient	Intolerant
Lonely	Irritable

Predominant Cravings:

- To Medicate
- To alter the mood (up or down)
- To create strong sensations in order to have the illusion one desires (security and power/control addictions, numb feelings, and sensations)

The Deep Secret of Sensation Addiction: The person feels disconnected and has a big empty space inside or an inner war. The person feels like a fake and cannot tolerate it; therefore, he or she must stimulate or sedate the mood and escape reality. In this state, the addict can have a lot of fun but no enjoyment.

The opposite of Sensation Addiction is our Divine Imprint of Enjoyment. Enjoyment is the ability to be fully in the "Now" moment connected to our feelings.

Characteristics of the Divine Imprint of Enjoyment

It is a radical shift in Self-Perception: *I am my true Identity*—happy, present, connected, satisfied, fulfilled, enthusiastic, joyful, and free. *I AM GLAD TO BE ME!*

The Beliefs and Imprints of Enjoyment are:

- I believe in the "Now" moment—living in the Power of Now
- I believe that pain is a teacher, love is the lesson, and suffering is optional
- I believe my happiness and fulfillment are a choice, an Inner job, and my responsibility
- I believe that to love is to enjoy

Predominant Identity Feelings for Enjoyment:

- Happy and Joyful
- Content and Grateful
- Enthusiastic and Trusting
- Excited and Peaceful
- Exalted and Serene
- Glad and Calm

Predominant Identity Behaviors:

- Rejoicing
- Appreciative
- Motivated
- Present
- Interested
- Enthusiastic
- Passionate
- Great Sense of Humor/Timing
- Patient
- Teachable

- Curious
- A Seeker

Predominant Identity Choices in the Imprint of Enjoyment:

- Self-actualization vs. instant gratification
- Self-actualization vs. intoxication
- Self-actualization and Creative Expression vs. depression
- Self-respect vs. cheap thrills
- Self-love vs. self-destruction
- Being fully present in the "Now" vs. past or future

Enjoyment is being Connected and in the Field. Enjoyment is being in the "Zone." It is being in the flow.

When you're in the flow:

- You have a clear vision of your purpose and know what to do
- You have the intuitive feeling of how well you're doing
- You feel engaged by the challenge, but not overwhelmed
- You're focused, confident, and relaxed
- You're fully absorbed by "Now" and the notion of time disappears

You can experience the "Zone" in sports, arts, or everyday work.
Enjoyment is BEING. It is freedom from Ego. A true paradigm shift.

Addiction To Suffering Vs. Creativity

Just as Enjoyment is the Divine Imprint and the opposite of Sensation Addiction, so Creativity is the Divine Imprint and opposite of Addiction to Suffering.

Characteristics of Addiction to Suffering

The Imprints for Addiction to Suffering are:

- Deep seated belief that life is hard and out to get you
- Deep seated belief in struggle/strife and bare survival
- **Trauma Bonding:** the person is defined by and bonded to the trauma of severe unrelenting trauma whether domestic violence, incest, or ritual abuse, and the trauma is replayed in their lives over and over
- Deep belief that suffering will attract sympathetic attention and validation

- Deep seated belief that one is trapped without choices
- Deep seated belief in the natural value system: an eye for an eye, a tooth for a tooth
- Deep seated belief in the futility of life; life and pain have no meaning

I recently saw a great cartoon depicting a conversation between a big dog and a small dog that perfectly illustrated the Addiction to Suffering. The big dog said, "I was thinking of all my problems…I was thinking of all the pain of the past and I was thinking of all the uncertainty of the future. Then I was thinking poor, poor me and my sad life; and then I was thinking how little time there is, and I am really thinking it's all just hopeless. What can I do?" The little dog replied, "Stop thinking!"

Usually, when we manage to stop thinking, we start hearing and feeling.

Addiction to Suffering is very different from Grief and Loss. Grief and Loss are legitimate feelings that need to be addressed and processed. It is also very different from Trauma Bonding, which needs to be addressed and treated or it will turn into the Addiction to Suffering. Addiction to Suffering is a profound belief in impossibilities and how "unlucky" one is. It is seeing life only through the eyes of Ego.

In my childhood, I saw many atrocities. I saw people suffer whose pain was legitimate, yet they had a creative resilience and a willingness to rise above their troubles. I have also seen people who possessed all the "ingredients" society says they need for happiness, yet they are miserable, bored, and suffering without any joy or meaning.

Victor Frankl, the father of logotherapy, wrote in his book *Man's Search for Meaning*, "Man's main concern is not to gain pleasure or to avoid pain, but rather to see a meaning in his life. That is why man is even ready to suffer, on the condition, to be sure, that suffering has a meaning."

Addiction to Suffering is suffering without a meaning. It is life viewed through the eyes of the Ego: no meaning, no solution, no choices, only a tunnel vision often coupled with cynicism.

Here is an example of addiction to suffering: In Tania's family, addictions run for generations. Tania's son was addicted to heroin. In spite of Tania's numerous attempts to have her son treated, he continued using. He was imprisoned due to drug possession. He was released from the penitentiary and went right back to using. He had no job, no money, and no car. He did not care to work. Tania continued to enable and bail out her son. She was giving him money, which he used for drugs. She fed him because he was out of money…he spent it on drugs. When Tania had no money, her son stole from her to get drugs. Tania continued doing the same thing over and over, expecting her son to "get it." Tania continued complaining, suffering, and repeating the insanity of codependence and enabling, in other words: "killing him softly with love."

Characteristics of the Divine Imprint of Creativity

The Divine Imprint of Creativity is truly the opposite of Addiction to Suffering. Our Creative Spirit animates a style of being, a lifetime filled with the desire to innovate and explore new ways of doing things. Creativity is bringing dreams to reality. It is the expression of our Identity that is our Authentic Self.

Life is meant to be expressed. Repression and suppression bring depression. The Law of Life is growth, expansion, and expression. All of the Universe is in constant creation.

Swami Beyondananda suggested, "Make a "*Not To Do List.*" Then don't do the items on your list. What if your "Not to Do List" included thinking the thoughts you no longer want to think? What strategy are you using to stop those thoughts?

Here is a powerful affirmation that works as a positive creative strategy to connect our heads to our hearts:

> *May the words of my mouth (thoughts) and the meditations of my heart (feelings) align for the highest and best expression in my world.*

When we do the things we most enjoy, we experience "re-creation." The word recreation means basically to create anew. It is the very impulse of life.

Our lives can be filled with creative moments whatever we do, as long as we are flexible, open, and receptive to new possibilities. We just have to be willing to step out of our comfort zone and be willing to try a new approach to old stuff.

Years ago, while I was creating the stained glass windows for Shaar Hashomayim Synagogue in Montreal, I had a problem. It had nothing to do with the design but with the technique. The theme of the windows was "The Burning Bush." We were using slab glass (3/4" to 1" thick glass) that was chipped with a hammer for the diffusion of light. My design of the flames contained reversed curves in the pieces, but with the thickness of the glass, that appeared impossible. I refused to believe it was impossible, so I convinced my partner to invent a saw that could cut the curves I needed. And the diamond saw for slab glass was born.

Creativity is expressed in cooking, lovemaking, parenting, and in living as well as in dying. My friend Jack was creative when he planned his own funeral service and invited all of his family and friends to participate. He creatively allowed a space for all of us to grieve, but more importantly, to bring closure. He taught many of us how to live and gave us a great lesson on how to transition from one plane of existence to another.

Everyone is capable of tapping into and accessing creative ideas. Creativity is not reserved for just a few. Creativity is the Life in each of us wanting to be more and to be expressed.

Therefore, this action step requires us to practice living a life of possibilities, visions, and creativity by aligning ourselves with our Divine Imprint. Just as the caterpillar surrenders to the imaginal cells of the butterfly, we surrender ego imprints and beliefs and rise to our true status as Spiritual Beings living our human experiences in a creative way. We are designed for excellence not mediocrity.

If right now, you feel you are hitting bottom, that your pain is so great that no solution is possible and you are at the best place to say, "Enough," then surrender now. Say out loud, "I surrender. I need help. I want to get well. I am ready and willing to do what it takes." Then watch the Universe respond. I know this works. I've been there, and I've seen thousands in the same place have their lives transformed. Surrender and trust. Love is on the way.

The Ninth Action Step To Transformation: Acceptance And Love...Love Is The Way

> "Love is the only sane and satisfactory answer to the problem of human existence."
>
> —Erich Fromm

Ego's imprint of Acceptance is very different from our Identity's imprints.

Ego Says: I accept you because I tolerate you
I accept you, provided you meet my expectations
I accept you, but I do not trust you

This conditional acceptance is not the kind of acceptance this action step talks about.

Acceptance Is: A mental attitude that something is believable and credible
An emotional state of approval and satisfaction
A Spiritual attitude of allowance, receptivity, and understanding

Acceptance is releasing my judgments and projections upon life while choosing over, and over, and over to LOVE WHAT IS!

With Acceptance, a powerful shift happens: we awake to new possibilities, and we deal with life and circumstances proactively. With this step, we begin accepting responsibility for our role in the world. With trust, and with openness and receptivity, we surrender to the calling of our Soul and our Authentic Self. We align our roles to our Authentic Self and our Soul. We give our Sacred Yes to our Life, and we are pulled higher by our Vision.

From Acceptance we go to Love. Love is one of the most misused words in our language. I love my husband and I love God, but I love chocolate too. A friend of mine used to joke that he loves humanity—it is people he cannot stand. Self-love is a practice in humility.

Denis Waitley said, "Happiness cannot be traveled to, owned, earned, worn or consumed. Happiness is the spiritual experience of living every minute with love, grace and gratitude."

Carl Jung said, "Where love rules, there is no will to power; and where power predominates, there love is lacking. The one is the shadow of the other."

And Paul Tillich defines love by saying, "The first duty of love is to listen."

A Course in Miracles teaches that we can listen to the voice of love or the voice of fear. It says, "Your divided devotion has given you two voices, and you must choose at which altar you want to serve."

> Infantile love follows the principle: "I love you because I am loved."
> Mature love follows the principle: "I am loved because I love."
> Immature love says: "I love you because I need you."
> Mature love says: "I need you because I love you."
>
> —Erich Fromm

So what kind of love are we talking about in this action? The ancient Greeks defined different types of love with different words, depending on the context in which the idea of love was used. Their words for love, in order of their degrees to the highest form of love, were: *philia, eros, storge, xenia, agape.*

Philia is:	A dispassionate virtuous love. It includes loyalty to friends, family, and community. It requires virtue, equality, and familiarity. Philia is motivated by practical reason; one or both of the parties benefit from the relationship.
Eros is:	Passionate love, with sensual desire and longing. The Greek word *erota* means love. In Greek mythology, Eros helps the soul recall knowledge of beauty and contributes to an understanding of spiritual truth. Lovers and philosophers are all inspired to seek truth in eros.
Storge is:	The love of a parent for a child.
Xenia is:	Hospitality. The love shown to a guest.
Agape is:	Charitable, selfless, altruistic, and unconditional Love. In most religions, it is the love of God.

Fig. 13-1: Types of Love According to the Ancient Greeks

For the Authentic Self, Agape Love is Energy. Love is the most powerful energy. It is an energy that creates, heals, transforms, attracts, blesses, prospers, and is unconditional. This action step refers to this kind of Love.

Now LOVE, genuine love, starts flowing. Love is the wisdom of an understanding heart, in which a new compassion for humanity and for ourselves is established. Our Authentic Self is Love. Our global heart is awakening: the heart that transcends cultures, races, religions, and all the dogmas that separate us. We start experiencing true Agape Love, Unconditional Love.

When we operate at this frequency of Love, we have a permanent understanding of our connection with all that exists. Our desire grows to reach out, to be more, to touch others, to serve, to participate and to make a difference in the world. As previously mentioned, Dr. David Hawkins calibrates love at 500.

At this frequency of Love, we operate with Purity of Intent, at a level where our knowledge, reason, talents, and skills are at the service of our heart for a greater good. Our sense of ethics, our sense of right and wrong (our conscience) are heightened. We are now creatively fulfilling our purpose. Our motives are pure and free of Ego. We look to serve humanity. Sadly, Dr. Hawkins estimates that only 1 in 250 people reach this level in their lifetimes.

We must be open to this transformation created by Love. As Dr. Martin Luther King Jr. said, "Love is the only force capable of transforming an enemy into a friend." That transformation has to start with us. When we give our Sacred Yes to our Authentic Self, Love is released. This kind of Love dissolves the power of our inner enemy, the Ego. Once that Love is released and we surrender to it, we become a loving power in the universe because we understand our oneness with all.

We are now living in an incredible time of human development—a quickening of consciousness is happening across the world. Out of the current chaos is emerging a new global heart anchored in compassion and a deep desire for a world that works for all.

The Ego structures of greed, power, dominance, and scare tactics are backfiring. Traditional politics no longer work. Nothing is going to work except for Love. *Love is the only power. Love is the healer. Love is who we are.*

> "There is no fear in love; but perfect love casts out fear."
> – 1 John 4:18 *NKJV*

As we accept this truth in an escalated way, this decade and this century will forever change the imprint of duality. Science as well as Spirituality will demonstrate the principle of ONENESS. Already, they are bridging the gap.

> "Eventually we come to understand that love heals everything, and love is all there is."
> —Gary Zukav

As A Result Of These Actions, We Will Experience: Oneness

The Oxford Pocket Dictionary defines Oneness as: "the state of being unified and whole, though comprised of two or more parts as the oneness of man and nature. Oneness is identity and harmony felt with all things. It is the fact or state of being one in number: belief in the oneness of God."

We can break down Oneness into four components we will explore individually:
- Integrity
- Alignment with the Energy of Love
- Alignment with Our Spiritual Nature
- Oneness with the Universe

Integrity

The first level of Oneness is Integrity. Integrity is an undivided or unbroken completeness or totality with nothing wanting. For us to have Integrity, it requires that what we think, what we feel, what we say, and what we do are one and congruent. Through the years, my imprints and Ego's fears were the big dividers in my life. What I thought and what I felt were more often than not incongruent. I might tell you one thing but do another. Through my clinical work, I have discovered that this incongruency is fairly common because our fears create a great divisive force within us. Achieving Oneness is about maturing and mastering fear.

> "Fear is the path to the dark side. fear leads to anger; anger leads to hate; hate leads to suffering."
> —Yoda, in *Star Wars: Episode IV - A New Hope (1977)*

These nine action steps teach us that we cannot have integrity as long as we have not conquered our fear. Nelson Mandela said it very well: "The brave man is not he who does not feel afraid, but he who conquers that fear." Plato wisely stated, "Courage...is knowing what not to fear" and "For a man to conquer himself is the first and noblest of all victories." The first level of Oneness, Integrity, means *Conquering our fears!*

Alignment with the Energy of Love

The second level of Oneness is aligning ourselves with the Energy of Love. Love is the unifying and harmonizing energy. When we truly start loving ourselves, our lives, and our world, we enter into a state of Oneness. The ninth action step said, "LOVE IS WHO WE ARE." Love is our Spiritual DNA, and Perfect Love casts away all fear. The result is that we now move to the next level.

Alignment with Our Spiritual Nature

The third level of Oneness is alignment with our Spiritual Nature. Our Oneness and connection as Spiritual Beings transcends language, culture, dogmas, and all self-imposed negative imprints. Love stretches us out of the comfort zone of our intellect and into our hearts where the world is mystical, inclusive, and creative. This level allows us to take ownership of our spirituality.

Spirituality allows us to recognize the illusion and falseness constructed by the Ego that has made us live in a mechanical, dream-like state. Spirituality awakens us to the Inner reality of our Authentic Self, which is vast, multidimensional, and already intimately connected with all of creation.

St. Gregory of Nyssa said it well: "Concepts create idols; only wonder understands anything." Religion is about certainty. Spirituality is about wonder. One divides; the other unifies. Albert Einstein explained this difference by observing, "The intuitive mind is a sacred gift and the rational mind is a faithful servant. We have created a society that honors the servant and has forgotten the gift."

Now we can return to the gift, the return to the intuitive mind. Our emotional intelligence, coupled with our intuitive mind, *Knows and Understands.*

In 2008, I encountered a creature in true alignment with its Spiritual Nature when my husband and I visited Mexico and had a chance to swim with the dolphins. The dolphin assigned to us was an eighteen-month old, 220-lb "baby" named Gondolpho. He was a beautiful and gentle creature. My heart ached because Gondolpho was on the job, yet I was grateful to experience being with him.

Gondolpho allowed us to embrace and caress him. I felt so connected to him. Then the trainer said Gondolpho would give us kisses. My husband half-jokingly asked the trainer whether dolphins ever bite humans, but before the trainer had a chance to respond, Gondolpho rose up out of the water in a vertical position and shook his head in a "No" pattern, emitting a sound that confirmed, "No." We were all astonished. We have an incredibly precious picture of Gondolpho gently kissing my husband—a true moment of Spiritual Alignment with Nature.

I also experienced that same feeling of Spiritual Alignment during my near-death experience when I was in the presence of the Being of Light. I then knew Perfect Love, Perfect Peace, and a total feeling of Belonging, Knowingness, and complete Freedom.

I had another experience of Spiritual Alignment in 1992 when a terminally ill dear friend and mentor wished to die in my arms. Witnessing his transition process was an honor and privilege as I held him; we experienced moments of tenderness and humor as people surrounded us whom he loved and who loved him. While seeing this strong man be reduced to a frail shadow of his former self touched my own vulnerability, far stronger was the feeling of Oneness because life and death are but one circle. It was an incredible chance to share the experience with spiritually like-minded people. It was a lesson in life, in death, and in fully assuming the final surrender of the breath of life. As we released him, others greeted him as his life went on into the next dimension.

Oneness with the Universe

The fourth dimension of Oneness concerns our entire planet. It is an awareness of our interdependence on all of life, a complete global awareness. Today, we are at a crossroads. As a civilization if we want to survive, we need to change all our imprints about leadership, about power, fear, and greed. Oneness is interdependence. We cannot continue our national games when we are a global community. Nor can we continue to ignore the rest of the planet while watching our self-indulgent "reality" shows.

In this new century and millennium, Oneness is a necessity. We need to transcend the world's divisions, its wars and self-destruction of our planet. In a century where our technology has surpassed our humanity, only our spirituality of Oneness can assure our existence. Oneness creates the inner marriage of our humanity with our Divinity.

In Oneness, we fully assume our roles as sons and daughters of a creative Universe. In Oneness, the mystical marriage of our energies takes place in our hearts; we become one with ourselves, with God/Love/Light/Universe—the terminology is not important; assuming responsibility for BEING IT is essential.

Peace cannot be kept by force. It can only be achieved by understanding.

When we achieve Oneness, we will have peace. We will finally know how to live freely.

> "We have before us the glorious opportunity to inject a new dimension of love into the veins of our civilization."
>
> Martin Luther King Jr.

14 Living in Freedom: Testimony

When we practice the Action Steps to Transformation to access the Authentic Self, we produce for ourselves a life of Freedom.

Our society has many concepts of what Freedom means. In general, Freedom is viewed as a state of not being imprisoned, enslaved, or otherwise constrained. Types of freedom include but are not limited to:

- Free will: the ability of rational agents to exercise control over actions, decisions, or choices
- Political freedom: the absence of interference with the sovereignty of an individual by the use of coercion or aggression
- Freedom of speech and expression
- Economic freedom
- Freedom of religion

The Action Steps to Transformation will produce an Inner Freedom from the imprisonment and coercion exercised by the Ego. Inner Freedom is the highest level of freedom because it changes our inner reality, thereby transforming how we experience our external reality.

When still in my early years of recovery, I was part of a group involved in bringing a recovery program into the Canadian Penitentiary Services. In those days, *my imprints of victimhood and "poor me"* were still active in my life. I was a prisoner of my own imprints.

In prison, I met Karl, a gentleman who formerly had been a chemist and held a very important position in life. He was serving a life sentence for killing two people with his car, driving intoxicated and while in an alcoholic blackout. Alcoholic blackouts are periods of amnesia when the level of alcohol consumption prevents the brain from forming memories.

Karl was thirty-six when he entered the penitentiary for life. Yet, the striking thing about him was his attitude that made him a free man, despite the prison walls. Karl had totally accepted his situation, even embraced his new circumstances and existence. Karl was at peace; he was a loving man surrounded by a world of anger and violence. He told me that in prison he had found a meaning and purpose in his life that had changed his imprint about life and freedom. He has devoted his life in prison to helping other inmates attain sobriety, forgiveness, and self-forgiveness. He became a role model of tolerance and serenity. To be at peace, whatever the circumstance, is to experience Freedom.

Throughout my life's work, I have come across many success stories of shifted imprints that allowed people to experience peace and freedom. Some of my friends have graciously agreed to share those stories here. Following are their stories of Recovery, Transformation, and ultimately, Freedom. I hope, along with my own story, they will serve as examples and new blueprints for you as you begin your own transformation of ridding yourself of your negative imprints, replacing them with positive ones, and ultimately, finding your Authentic Self and the Freedom that accompanies that discovery.

Freedom from Religious and Cultural Imprints (Lila)

As a small child, my soul intuitively knew I was connected to a powerful Source. However, I did not have a conscious awareness that I was a privileged child of God's Universe while my parents were just custodians of my body. But my soul has always known who it really is. I believe that is why I was born into the family I experienced in this lifetime.

I am a female child born into a high profile Muslim family. I always sensed that I was disconnected from the strong ethnic, cultural, and religious foundation in which I was born and lived; later, I realized that foundation became the blueprint for the imprints of my life's path.

As a Muslim child and young woman, I internalized the message that I was expected to be "perfect" in every way, which included integrity of the highest order, physically, mentally, emotionally, and spiritually. I was expected to perform at higher levels than most people without any mistakes or misgivings; this expectation gave birth to *my imprint: I must be perfect and compete with everyone*, which in turn prevented my ability to feel I belonged or to be fulfilled. Later in my life, I would discover how imprints override our thoughts and without a doubt our dreams.

My environment did not provide me with the emotional, intellectual, and Spiritual guidance and support I needed to achieve this perfection; it was just assumed I should know how to be and how to do what was expected without directions. The overall message I internalized from this culture and from the Muslim world was that I had to be rigorously honest, loving, generous, and "without faults" and in exchange, one day God would allow me go to Heaven, after all of my deeds were reviewed by God's board of directors.

Any number of people would think, that with such high expectations and programming, my imprint would register for me to be as much like God as possible.

However, in my culture and religion, to be created in the image and likeness of God was specifically reserved for the male culture. A woman would only be considered worthy if she were to obey all the requirements that her father, brothers, uncles, and husband placed upon her. Therefore, that God would ever love a sweet, smart, and beautiful little girl like me felt like an illusion that could never happen; this realization set into place the roadmap and foundation for self-limitations, rejection, abandonment, and addictions. Growing up, I internalized my environment's message to be superior although its foundation was anchored in dysfunction, unmet needs, unrealistic expectations, and an environment that could turn violent when least expected. Years later, I realized it was a karmic imprint that would take me on a journey of darkness and light.

Once I had internalized my culture and religion's messages and imprints, they became my negative belief system. I saw myself as not "good enough," "smart enough," or "honest enough." I had the deep feeling that I did not accomplish enough, and I did not have enough of anything. I was out of alignment with my soul but did not understand that or know how to reverse it at the time. Today, I know that if my life is not aligned with my soul, I can never be enough to others or myself.

My reality was that the "perfect home" in which I had grown up was built upon the DNA of many generations of abandonment, neglect, and pain. At first examination, I was not conscious of my intuition as a guiding light for my life's purpose. In retrospect, my intuition became my strongest asset for survival and knowing how to survive the tsunami of double messages with waves of rejection, fear, anger, and despair. Finally, my spiritual bankruptcy led me to Pavillon Gilles Desjardins in Canada; that experience changed the trajectory of my life.

Gilles and Liliane and their staff understood at the soul level that people are flawless when the Ego is surrendered and the Soul's identity has a chance to emerge. When I arrived at Pavillon, I knew I was in the right place. I believe I knew at the cellular level when I was guided to Montreal that it would be the journey of a lifetime. As I presented my "perfect spiritually bankrupt self" to the Desjardins, I was taken by the hand and heart to meet the sweet soul that would have the courage to rewrite the script of her own life—myself. I was guided through sessions of Twelve-Step work, reality therapy, and most importantly, Soul Imprint work.

The Soul Imprint work was my emancipation. I discovered that the new imprints I set in place were audible, powerful, and the road map to my greatest gifts. I came to realize that the environment where I grew up was the gift that would allow me to experience the beauty of men, women, and children.

Today, I no longer view spiritual perfection in a religious context through the eyes of pain and abandonment. For me, spiritual perfection is no longer reserved only for the male gender, nor is it coming from authority figures and set by the illusory mold of fear. Today, I know and feel the inclusiveness of being one with men, women, and children, and that no one person is more or less superior than the next. Today, I know we are all connected to the same source no matter what religion, faith, or practice we believe and follow.

I have walked through the dark night of the soul only to understand that darkness and light require the same skills. Today, I have skills I learned as a result of my confusing childhood; I know the strength of my endurance and the strength of my resilience as well as the level of my integrity; those skills have become the foundation of my professional success.

The compassion I have for my family today is directly rooted in the love and guidance I needed as a child but did not get. Now I no longer separate men, women, and children as superior or inferior, but as souls on the path of love and forgiveness.

I believe the greatest strength my negative childhood imprints gave me is the ability to forgive. Forgiveness is my foundation to love. Today, I can measure the amount of love, forgiveness, and fulfillment I experience when I realize that some of my most valuable thoughts and feelings come from the Muslim home in which I grew up. Now I have the ears to hear and eyes to see the source of that inspiration. God, love, and guidance can come from many sources. My Muslim roots have their inspiration in Islam, which says, "If you hurt the leaf of a tree, you have hurt the soul of mankind." There is peace, love, and forgiveness, and they come from places that are familiar to us only if we are willing to break the chains of erroneously imprinted beliefs and patterns. Today I know that love, forgiveness, and peace are not reserved to the texts of Quran, Bible, or Torah, but are a living moving muscle in my heart and soul because God is my personal and loving friend, partner, CEO, CFO, and mentor, with angels who deliver and demonstrate beauty to me daily. For that I am truly grateful. This awareness is the cornerstone of my maturity and my freedom.

Freedom from Eating Disorder and Codependency (Diana)

I was raised in the South by a beautiful mother who had a model-thin body. She had been the homecoming queen and was very popular in our town. My dad, on the other hand, was on the chubby side, and I have inherited his looks. Everyone admired my mom, and my dad kept telling me how I needed to look like Mom.

Throughout my childhood, Mom controlled my meals. She would make comments like, "You're putting on weight; no one will like you, nor be interested in you; you must be careful." Her favorite comment when I would put on a dress I liked was, "On you, this dress looks like it belongs to your baby sister." *My imprint was: I am ugly, I am huge and I am unlovable.*

The more rejected I felt, the more I tried to lose weight. By twelve years old, I was anorexic and codependent. My entire value came from others; they had the power to accept or reject me.

My body image was totally distorted. Even when I became anorexic, I could not see the weight loss that happened. Nor could I understand why my mother was suddenly jealous of me, or why my father was paying more attention to me. My anorexia progressed. At fourteen, I was hospitalized and in bad physical shape.

I underwent lengthy treatment for anorexia, but I did not change my imprint that I was ugly and unlovable. I only learned how to manage the anorexia.

I got married at eighteen. I went for the first guy who paid attention to me. He had the full power to make or break me. I was so codependent. I repressed all my needs, and I focused only on his. I was going to be the best wife; I felt so grateful that somebody loved me. As I was rejecting my body, I was rejecting my sexuality too. Our sex life was not satisfying to him, and it did not take very long for him to get tired of me and look for excitement elsewhere. I was convinced it was because I was ugly and unlovable.

During our divorce, I went from anorexia to bulimia to obesity. Finally, one day I woke up and got help. This time I had a chance to look at my imprints and belief systems. As I did the steps, I totally changed my self-perception as well as my body image. Now I am my healthy and normal weight. My body no longer defines me. I love my life and myself.

Today, I am in a healthy relationship and I have solid boundaries for my ego. Whenever my ego wants to start feeding me lies about myself and how I must people-please, care take, be a martyr, and look perfect, I surrender and get re-connected with my Authentic Self. I remember who I am. My sexual life is free of my old imprints, and I have my permission to enjoy it freely. Needless to say, my partner is the beneficiary of my freedom. I am sometimes surprised by all the blessings and love in my life—it seems like it was another life that I lived before. Every day, I am grateful for my peace and my newfound freedom.

Freedom from Destructive Parenting Imprints (Gerry)

I am the father of three boys and a girl. My family is a "normal" family. For years while I ran a successful business, my wife was home; she raised the children and was involved in their schools and in our church. People who looked at us used to tell me, "You are so lucky."

Well on the outside yes, I was lucky, but on the inside it was different. My children avoided me; they did not want to talk to me. First, I just thought they were busy with school; then they were gone to college. Not until my oldest son got married and had his first child did I realize something was truly wrong. My son did not want his child to be near me. That hurt. So one day when my children were all visiting, I asked them to tell me what was wrong.

To my great surprise, they told me. "Dad, you were never there for us. When you were, you were running this home like your board meeting. You were barking orders at us. You never encouraged us. No matter how much we succeeded, it was never enough for you."

My oldest son, with tears in his eyes, said to me, "Do you remember the day I scored my first home run? I was so happy. No, you were not at the game; I was used to that. I came home all excited to tell you the news. You started shouting at me; you called me by my brother's name and asked me when I would grow up and start taking life seriously instead of wasting my time on baseball. To you it did not matter what any of us needed, wanted, or loved. To you, it was your way or the highway. As long as you provided, your job was done. I don't know you, Dad. I have nothing to talk about with you. You never told me what you're afraid of. You never shared what is really meaningful to you. When we were sick, you were on the phone or gone. When we succeeded at anything, you were not there to cheer us on. We don't know you, Dad. Who are you besides being the CEO? Who are you, Dad, besides the orders that you scream? I do not want my child to be barked at. I want my child to feel safe. We never did."

When my son was finished speaking, all of my children left. My wife went to her den, and I was left to think. My son's words hurt to the core, and I realized that I had missed the boat. I decided to go get some help on parenting. I knew how to run a company. I had no clue on how to be a father, much less a dad.

I ended up in treatment listening to so many similar stories. I realized that I did to my children what I had been taught by my father. Dad had been an army general, and his children had been his private little army. He barked orders; he did not have time for "feelings"—that was women's stuff. Dad was taking care of "real" and "serious" business.

My imprint of parenting was: A father is a provider and cannot be bothered with raising the kids; that is the wife's job. A father needs to give orders. You don't tell your children what they did well or they will become boastful. To be obeyed, you must keep your distance.

That day I cried. I realized that I hadn't known my father; we were never close. I can't tell you whether he was happy or miserable; I can't tell you what were his hopes and dreams. The worst part was that he was dead. He was gone, so I would never know him now. At the same time, I realized I did not know my children either.

In treatment, I put down on paper my values, my dreams, my hopes, my regrets, and my gratitude. I wrote pages and realized how love is the one gift that needs to be given now. I wrote letters to all my children, I asked for their forgiveness; I told them things about me that I never knew were there. I asked them to reveal themselves to me. I did not want to die and be known as the CEO; I wanted to be a dad and a granddad. My children and my wife came to my family week. I was not an "Addict" like the substance addicts. My disease was my emotional unavailability, my need for control, and my fear of vulnerability. My wife did a tremendous job with our children. They felt courageous enough to tell me the truth. I took it; I changed. *My new imprint is: I am a Daddy. A Daddy understands, supports, loves, discloses his vulnerabilities, admits his mistakes, is present and teaches by example.*

Now in our home, everyone is free to be who he or she really is. My grandkids run to me, and I tell them stories of how great their parents are. It is never too late. Love changes everything and brings freedom to all.

Freedom from the Infamous "They" (Irene)

My parents emigrated from Poland/Russia to Canada in the early 1900s as pre-teens. The community was mainly made up of immigrants from Poland, Ukraine, and Russia and all had small farms. My parents both attained third grade educations before they left school to work—my father on the family farm and my mother as a housekeeper. My father was twenty-six and my mother sixteen when they married. *My imprint was: Education isn't important. You don't need education to be a farmer's wife.*

My life in this world started off rocky. A child previously born to my parents died at three months old and my mother was blamed for his death—she was too young, too weak. The fear of losing another child dominated her life, not only during pregnancy, but during parenting. Her fear resulted in her parenting me with tight reins. *My imprints were: The world is not a safe place and because of that you must control everything and everybody.*

School was rough. Because of the imprints of not needing education, I wasn't motivated to learn, but I wasn't encouraged either. I remember one time needing help with my homework. I can even remember feeling charged up with what I was learning. I asked my mother to help me; however, she couldn't. She didn't have a clue what I was asking her about, and she blew it off by telling me all those things weren't important. What was important for me was to learn how to cook, clean house, look after chickens, and be a good wife. I quit school after eleventh grade and went to work as a receptionist. I had just turned seventeen. That was a tough year; I was clueless about what to do, and because of my sheltered life in a culturally tight community, I had never encountered a "receptionist" at work. That job lasted only a year before I was "laid off"—at least, that's what I was told.

That year seems to be a blur to me—I think it's because I was in a state of total confusion. I moved from a small, tight-knit culturally based community into another culture. Nothing was the same as what I was used to. The culture I moved into was "English" and the community I came from didn't speak well of them. They were those infamous "they" who were doctors and lawyers, owned businesses, held government positions, lived in expensive homes, and ate in expensive restaurants. *My imprints were: Who do they think they are? It must be nice to have so much money. They are smarter than you because they are educated. You are not good enough.*

I wasn't out of a job for long because I was immediately hired by a government employment agency. The staff obviously saw potential in me because I was trained to be a counselor, a job I worked at for five years. During that time, I married (and no, he wasn't a farmer.) Then an opportunity came up for me to buy a business. At twenty-two, I became the owner of a successful flower shop. I had mixed emotions;

on one hand I was happy to become one of the infamous "they," but on the other hand, the imprints of "Who do they think they are?" caused me emotional chaos.

Because I loved being an entrepreneur, I quickly expanded the business by buying another store and setting up six agents in the community. During the same time, I became the first female president of the Chamber of Commerce in northern Alberta. As well, I was a board member of the Northern Development Board. Not bad for a farmer's daughter with only an eleventh grade education. However, the nagging imprint of not being good enough resulted in inner turmoil, which was heightened by my mother one day saying to me, "Who do you think you are? You aren't as smart as they are." There we go again, being compared to the infamous "they," and as a beaten child would feel, I really felt I wasn't good enough to be as successful as I had become.

After six years, I sold the businesses and attempted to be a stay at home mom. I was going to fulfill my role in life by being a wonderful wife and mother. I think the next two years were the most confusing ones of my life. Yes, I was a good cook and kept the house clean. I was even involved with the kids at school by volunteering and being president of the PTA. But I was totally bored. There was nothing to stimulate my mind. I didn't enjoy the role of being a housewife, so I decided I needed to go back to work.

I was immediately hired by the police force and put in charge of administrative functions for the complete subdivision, which encompassed Northern Alberta. During my eleven years with the force, my duties changed and I became involved with the forensics and undercover departments. As well, I was the police force's EAP (Employee Assistance Program) officer for Northern Alberta. I also had an opportunity to take much training, get my GED, and start an undergraduate program, paid for by the government.

Placed in a position of much authority, my imprints of power and control took over in full force (pun intended!). I truly learned that the world is not a safe place, so what better place to work than a place of authority, especially when I was "the" authority.

From a very young age, I was interested in the "something more" to life. I didn't know what that "more" was because my religious upbringing had taught me only that God was to be feared. (In fact, every time it thundered, it was a sign that God was angry.) My searching led me to studying metaphysics on my own. I was enthralled with hands-on-healing and started taking out-of-town workshops/ training. My newfound interest was my best-kept secret because my friends and family would not have approved of it. *My imprint: You mustn't tell anyone about what goes on in the family. What will the neighbors say?*

However, my opportunity came into full-bloom when my husband and I moved 3,000 miles away to a place where no one knew us. To me, the move felt like I was starting the first day of the rest of my life because I could do anything I wanted to do without being shunned or criticized. I took training and became a Licensed

Massage Therapist. I finally had an umbrella that provided me with legal coverage to touch and do hands-on-healing. My practice exploded in popularity, and by constantly taking workshops and training, I was introduced to many healing modalities, including hypnosis, which I used with my clients.

But successful as my new career was, I still had the nagging imprint of "not being good enough" because I lacked an academic background. I enrolled at a local university to complete the undergraduate program I had started with the police force and graduated *summa cum laude* with a Bachelor of Liberal Studies. My tract was psychology, giving me the license to practice Psychosynthesis. A combination of still not feeling I was "good enough" and an enjoyment of studying made me decide to pursue my Master of Arts in Psychology and I graduated with a 4.0 GPA. Finally, I was able to prove I wasn't as stupid as my parents had told me; at least, that was one attempt to changing the imprint. I also taught classes at a local college—something I had long dreamed of doing.

Immediately after we moved and settled in our new surroundings, my husband and I were guided to a non-denominational church that worked for us because spirituality was its base. I finally found there what I was looking for—a God who is Love. I also met Liliane and Gilles, and to make a long story short, I attended Pavillon International in Val David, Quebec. It was a life-changing experience for me and my biggest "Aha!" was realizing that all the imprints passed down by my parents (and generations before them) to me had shaped how I lived my life. I had no idea that how I behaved, acted, thought, and reacted were actual imprints and that I could rewrite the script. How liberating was that! I got in touch with my identity, a part of me I hadn't been consciously aware of before.

After twelve years in the healing field, I felt I was "done." I had proven to myself that I wasn't stupid, and I'd had an opportunity to guide others to a place of healing, a passion that burned inside me. I took a three-year sabbatical while writing and publishing my memoir. That whole writing experience was very cathartic and very rewarding. Not only did my book win awards, but many of its readers indicated that my story had changed their lives. At this time, I also started doing genealogy. It seemed like part of me still wanted to dig into my past generations to learn who those people really were and how their lives were an influence on my imprints.

While researching the publishing industry, I realized a need existed that wasn't filled. Bringing my entrepreneurial skills to the forefront, I created an online company. However, this time was very different. This time I decided I was going to walk my talk. I was going to hand over the business to God and claim God as the company's CEO. The day I turned it over to God, and really meant and felt it, the business exploded. Within two months, I was hiring staff because I couldn't handle it by myself. But, there is more. I asked God to give me direction on the next steps and diligently listened for the direction. Since the declaration, which was almost five years ago, I've created six successful online businesses, have one full-time and one part-time staff, four virtual assistants, eight contractors, and over forty volunteers. And, you know what? I don't have a business plan! I've never been asked by God to create one, and I really don't see a need for one. After all, the CEO of the company has a plan. I just have to show up.

As well, I have to show up for life—my life. The negative imprints are still there, but I don't have to succumb to them. I have a choice and the choice is to create new imprints:

- *The world within is a safe place. I choose to live my life in love.*
- *I am good enough. I have all my needs met and my wants fulfilled.*
- *I express my thoughts in a loving manner. My words express love.*
- *I am a loving wife and mother. My clean home isn't who I am.*

Freedom from Self-Loathing (Mark)

I was around four years old when I knew on some deep, intrinsic level of my being that I was different from everybody else, and that I had to hide this differentness as best I could because it was definitely not good. In fact, I knew, without anyone ever telling me, that it was bad…very bad. I didn't know that I was gay then because I didn't know that word, nor did I necessarily feel attracted to men. What I did feel was more like a girl on the inside and a boy on the outside. I wanted to play dolls, jump rope, and skip around with the girls, but where I was from, a blue-collar city outside of Detroit, the rules for how boys and girls were to act and present themselves were narrow and clearly divided—no room for gray areas. Boys played with boys and did boy things like climb trees, play sports, wrestle, and were into cars, trucks, hunting, and fishing. Girls, well, they did girl things, of course. I was stuck in the middle. I can remember thinking something was terribly wrong. Did God play a joke on me? Did he intend for me to be a mistake?

That was one of the first imprints: "I am a mistake." God made a mistake and *I am it*. At the ripe old age of four, or perhaps even a bit younger, I made a decision—not a conscious one, but one that would forever alter my experience of life. Being that I was a mistake, I decided I had to put my fabulousness (as I call it today), my passion and my true identity on the shelf, locked in the closet. I had to hide my dirty secret for the sake of belonging. I needed desperately to belong, as we all do as young children. However, the fact that I needed to pretend to be somebody other than who I was in order to fit in obviously meant that I did not… and I would not… fit in. That was my second deep, traumatic imprint: *"I don't belong."*

With these two imprints packed into my lunch box, I started kindergarten. I remember being so afraid to go that I sobbed and clung desperately to my mother, begging her not to leave me. Did I on a subconscious level know that this first day of school would be the beginning of thirteen long, painful, lonely years? That would explain the hysteria and irrational fear that consumed me as I looked around through my tears watching other children laughing, playing, and easily leaving their parents to embark upon this new adventure.

School was hell. Although I tried with everything I had in me to be like the other boys, I wasn't fooling any of the other kids. Children are very smart because they are able to see the truth and are not afraid to speak directly to it. They are also sponges for their parents' fears, judgments, and homophobia. I was horrifically picked on and threatened on a daily basis. Hardly was there a day when at least one person didn't call me "faggot," "sissy," "gay lord,"—you name it, I was called it. Often the class bullies would threaten to beat me up after school, which scared me to death, making me obsess for the entire day about how to get out of school quickly so I could run home as fast as I possibly could. Fortunately, they were mostly idle threats, but there was more than one occasion where they weren't idle and I had to run for—what felt like—my life.

I was recently asked by a friend, "Did you ever fight back? Why didn't you stand up for yourself?" I told her, "I never thought to fight back. They were right. I *was* a faggot, a sissy, and gay. They saw my secret shame and ridiculed me and ruthlessly attacked it. I had no defense...they were right!" So instead of fighting, I swallowed my pain, swallowed their hatred, and internalized it all.

To add to the trauma, I was also sexually abused when I was around six years old. I blocked out the entire experience until I was around twenty-five when it all came to me in a flashback. I had heard of people who were sexually abused but had no memory. That sounded ridiculous to me. How could that be possible? Well, I personally found out it is possible...very possible. It's actually a brilliant choice for the mind completely to block out trauma in service to survival.

Some of the other primary negative imprints, along with the two previously mentioned, that I acquired from the trauma of being sexually abused, both overtly and covertly, and from growing up in a homophobic society are:

- *Self-hatred*

- *Sexual shame (includes desires, fantasies, masturbation, any sexual act)*

- *Sexual orientation shame (which is not about the act of sex, but about my homosexual identity)*

- *I am not enough*

- *I am deeply flawed*

- *I am invisible/do not matter*

In order to fit in and belong, I had to cover up these imprints as best as I could. Truth be told, I didn't know they were even there. I just became an expert at lying, presenting myself as who you would like me to be instead of who I really was, and escaping into a fantasy world where I was famous, successful, and powerful, causing everyone who once ridiculed me to worship and bow down to me. Dramatic? Sure, but it was what got me through a very rough, lonely, and scary childhood.

I was a sophomore in college when the first crack in my protective armor happened, which caused me to feel the enormous pain from these imprints like I had never felt before. I was in my first relationship. Paul and I were deeply, deeply in love...or so I thought. Truth be told, I was obsessed with him. A fear I had never known before gripped me, causing me often to feel insecure and certain that he would leave me for another. I was desperate and in horrible pain. I felt so inadequate, unsure, and vulnerable. I gave my soul away to this relationship. The scariest point was in the summer between my junior and senior year when I couldn't get the thoughts of suicide to stop racing through my mind. I sought the help of a therapist who told me that, according to his expert opinion, I was addicted to Paul—I was a relationship addict. I wasn't nearly ready to realize what that truly meant and how it was really impacting my life. Instead of moving toward recovery, I stopped seeing that therapist and instead allowed myself to become more and more consumed by the relationship.

When Paul and I graduated from college, we moved to Chicago to pursue our dreams. He was going to be a big advertising executive, and I was going to become a successful performer. My older brother and my father helped us move. When they departed, I remember looking at the huge city around me and I wept—very much like I did the first day of kindergarten. I felt alone, scared, and unequipped to be an adult, live on my own, and become whom I had always dreamed of being.

The good news was that the relationship addiction I was experiencing with Paul started to subside. The bad news was that the reason it was subsiding was because it was being replaced by sex addiction. As Paul went off to work, I was supposed to go to my dance lessons, voice lessons, acting classes, and find an agent. Instead, I started acting out sexually with strangers—almost every day. I felt so powerless over Paul most of the time, but when I was pursuing sex or having it with strangers, I felt powerful, in my body, alive and free. Before I knew it, the sex had me. What began as a once in awhile fling quickly became a daily drug I had to have. The imprints of "I'm not enough," "I'm a mistake," and add to those "phony, afraid, and unworthy" are not a great foundation for the confidence needed to pursue a career in…well…anything, really! My dreams and goals quickly fell to the wayside as all my energy and attention went more and more down the dark road of sex addiction.

They say it is darkest before the dawn, and in my case it was true. At the height of the insanity, I was having sex sometimes up to five times a day, all with different people. I was lying to Paul, jeopardizing his and my health, and falling more and more deeply into despair. I no longer knew who I was. Every morning, I made a list of things to do that would move my "career" forward, but instead, I would waste yet another day immersed in sex addiction. To so many friends and acquaintances, I was this nice, innocent, happy guy with the world before me. Inside, I was a liar, insecure, a cheat, selfish, narcissistic, and frozen in fear. Fortunately for me, it didn't take long for the two worlds to crash together, causing me to fall to my knees for the first time in a long prayer. I felt God within me—for lack of a better term—and I felt guided to call a dear friend I had known since I was around fifteen years old. Although I hadn't seen her for years, Tracey was one of my best friends. I called her up and told her everything—that I was acting out sexually and couldn't stop, that I was trapped in this relationship, and most importantly, that I felt like I was killing myself.

Unbeknownst to me, she had joined Alcoholics Anonymous herself about one year earlier. She had heard of sexual addiction and told me there were meetings in Chicago that I could attend. She told me I would meet other people with the same problem and they could and would help me, if I would let them.

It was a miracle! I went to my first Twelve-Step meeting for sexual addiction the next day. Only two other people were there, but the three of us had a meeting. They told me their stories, and for the first time, I deeply related. They told me about how they were living double lives and couldn't stop. They talked about their pain and suffering, and they talked about a solution—a way out. I immediately knew I belonged there.

It was at a Twelve-Step recovery weekend retreat where the flashbacks of being sexually abused flooded over me for the first time. I was absolutely in shock. I didn't know where to go or who to turn to, so again I fell to my knees in prayer. Dear friends of mine from the church I belonged to helped me to go to the Pavillon recovery center outside of Montreal, Canada. I believe that spending a month in this spirit-filled place, surrounded by people who did what they did from the deepest place of love, is what rescued me from what would have been an inevitable path of destruction. It was at Pavillon that I started to see the imprints of shame and fear that were driving my addictions and literally ruining my life. It was also at Pavillon where I was shown the magnificent, perfect being who was inside me.

I wish that simply seeing our magnificent Self were enough for us to begin living from it all the time. That wasn't my experience. Pavillon set me on the right path, but the path stretched before me with many twists and turns. For the next several years, right up to today, I attended countless Twelve-Step meetings, saw a handful of brilliant therapists when needed, read several books, and attended retreats and workshops all geared toward helping me love myself, accept life on life's terms, and surrender my beliefs, surrender my fears, surrender everything that blocked me from the God of my being.

Today, I am forty-five and my life is nothing like I thought it would be...it is much better. The imprints from my childhood that caused so much pain and suffering, that blocked me from showing up authentically in my career, relationships, and pretty much every area, are still there, but they no longer run my life. Instead, if I may risk being cheesy, they are more like my friends. When I feel the imprints of not belonging, believing I am a mistake, deep shame, and fear becoming activated, I am now able to breathe, feel them, and even talk about them in the moment they are occurring. They guide me back to center and help me to take better care of myself.

The true miracle is that the two areas in my life that I could not get to work, relationships and career, are now the areas that bring me my greatest joy and fulfillment. I am in a fourteen-year relationship with a man I love and respect, and with whom I am learning and growing. That's not to say we don't have our challenges, but what we have far beyond challenges is God in the center of the relationship and a commitment to share, tell our truth, and support each other to be the best people we can be in and out of our coupleship. In terms of my career, God is using my gifts and talents in a way I would never, ever, ever have imagined. I am a minister, the founder of the Bodhi Spiritual Center in Chicago, which is a thriving, diverse, hip, real, and deep spiritual community dedicated to revealing love, honoring all paths, and celebrating life! I am an author, international speaker, and carry a personal mission of helping to heal the world of homophobia. I am fulfilled, grateful, and know I make a difference in other people's lives.

The tools I use to help me become free from these imprints are prayer, meditation, forgiveness, spiritual community, honesty, Twelve-Step work, surrender, self-acceptance, and patience...lots of patience. One might say, "Wow, that's a lot of work! When do you have time to live your life and have fun?" To which I reply, "This is my life, and I'm probably more surprised than you to say, 'It is fun.'" It's work too, and it's deep, important, fulfilling, and worth all the hours, days, months, and years. I believe that "for this I have come." I have come here, this lifetime, to cleanse my consciousness of every false belief and all negative imprints, and then to help those who are seeking the same kind of freedom to do the same.

It is an amazing journey filled with grace...amazing grace.

Freedom from Fear (Charles)

That particular year, the North Carolina Medical Board chose to have its quarterly meeting at an elegant Raleigh hotel conference center. The ambiance was collegiate and the attire was formal. Only miles from my familiar Duke University Medical Center, I felt appropriately dressed, yet totally nude. I was damp and nauseatingly nervous as I waited for my audience in the lobby. I could tell this would be another "life-defining" moment. The mental noise was deafening, but I managed to feel my physician-mentor's grip. "It's time," he said. "Your name has been called twice."

As we walked upstairs and toward the principal review room, doors, some open, some ajar, revealed glimpses into cubicles where individual doctors sat before one or two interviewers. At the end of the hallway, I was ushered into a spacious boardroom that I entered in a deliberately stoic manner, attempting to appear composed. I was directed to one end of a large polished table and sat in a high-back leather chair before a microphone wired to a cassette recorder. The Medical Board president introduced himself, the Board attorney, and then the five physician members sitting clockwise from him; they all looked at me intently while nodding politely in my direction as their names were announced. I was informed that all proceedings were being recorded, and I voiced my acknowledgment. I swallowed silently, took a deep breath, and proceeded to tell my story.

Following a brief relapse, I had recently returned from my second alcohol and cocaine dependency treatment in sixteen months. The most recent was a four-month program designed specifically for physicians by Doctor Doug Talbott, a world-renowned psychiatrist and addictionist. I emphasized the intensity and proven efficacy of this rehabilitation center. In an equally rehearsed fashion, I reassured the Board that "this time" my recovery was "sure-footed." It was the un-rehearsed portion at the end of my speech that caught, even me, by surprise: "And by the way...while I was away... I tested positive for HIV and Hepatitis C." A long uncomfortable silence followed. I could barely believe my public revelation; after all, I had tested anonymously; this was supposed to be my most personal secret! However, it was no longer mine to keep. Dr. Talbott's memorable lecture on addictions still rings in my ears—"Within Your Secrets Lies Your Illness." After fourteen years of university preparation and medical training, my practice of medicine was about to change dramatically.

Months later, I was told that I had been the first surgeon to inform the North Carolina Medical Board of his HIV positive status. Unfortunately, many others would follow. Two decades plus later, I'm still recovering from and marveling at life. But this story should restart with my childhood for it is there that some major beliefs were planted that would control my life for many years to come. *My imprints were: Fear and insecurity, accepting responsibility for others' feelings and*

emotions, being different, being not enough, and a chronic shameful state that made
me undeserving of all goodness no matter how hard I worked.

I was born on Colombia's Caribbean Coast in 1957. Located on the banks of the
massive Magdalena River, my birthplace, Barranquilla, remains an important
oceanic and river port. The city is also home to one of the oldest international
airports in South America. My childhood home was spacious and located in the
desirable El Prado neighborhood. Most memorably, it was constructed around a
large tiled courtyard surrounded by open Moorish-arched breezeways. Hanging at
each archway were massive ferns interspaced with lone canaries or finch-filled
wood and wire cages. The backyard was replete with mango, tamarind, and guava
trees; under a large acacia stood a colorful palm thatched, white-washed structure
that served as the servants' quarters. Gustavito, my best friend, lived there. He was
only three years my senior, but I always perceived him as much older. He was
brave, tall, and strong, and he always greeted me with a huge ivory smile, as if he
had not seen me for weeks though it had only been hours. We were inseparable; we
collected beetles and butterflies, and we even climbed the trees on Sundays after
Mass. We were constantly in search of the most perfect and fast guava worm to
submit at our neighborhood's weekly caterpillar races; we almost always won.
Beyond friends, we shared a special bond; we often communicated silently by
bumping bare shoulders, exchanging intense eye contacts, nods, and smiles. The feel
of our interlaced fingers, as we made mud-pies following a heavy downpour, would
place me in a trance-like state. More than once, the adults took notice and
expressed their concerns. "Boys shouldn't sit so close together," my mother would
say. "Go climb trees; boys shouldn't play kitchen," my visiting aunt would echo.
Though only a child of six, these remarks made me feel "different" in a very
uncomfortable way. *My imprints were: There is something wrong with you; you are*
not enough.

Gustavito and his baby brother lived in the colorful garden dwelling along with
their mother, Carmenza. She was a stout Caribbean mulatta who ruled over house
and garden matters with posture and her mostly silent authority. She directed her
assistants in minute detail, tailored to my mother's wishes. I was convinced
Carmenza was magically endowed so that everything she touched became special—
from the family meals to my starched school shirts. Her skin gleamed like polished
mahogany, and she always carried the sweet scent of coconut oil, as if she had just
stepped out of the shower. I was certain that the canaries sang and the turpiales
whistled at her whim.

My mother was also amazing in her own way. She remains a beautiful, loving
woman, but she has been profoundly affected by her own father and her husband's
alcoholism. When I was a child, she would hug and kiss me on every possible
occasion—expressions of affection she did not receive in her own childhood. She
was the first-born to one of the wealthiest families in the state of Bolivar, so my
mother became accustomed to a showering of material goods as demonstrations of

affection instead of hugs and kisses. Her personal dreams were quelled by the customs of the times. My mother wanted to become a bacteriologist or a famous lawyer like her uncles; instead, she was directed to become a "polished" lady at the exclusive *La Presentacion*, a Catholic boarding academy in Cartagena. Though only a few miles from her own home, she was allowed to visit only during the holidays. Instead of her wishes for a college education, she settled for finishing school and a long chaperoned tour of Europe's cultural and arts centers. Upon her return at seventeen, she fell in love with an arranged suitor; a handsome dark haired Scotsman with piercing sky-blue eyes, he was Barranquilla's societal catch and soon would become my father. On her wedding day, my mother was escorted to the Imaculada Concepcion Cathedral riding in the limousine of her uncle, the governor. A large entourage assisted with her one-of-a kind Italian tailored gown; it was all quite grand and the newspaper's society pages documented the entire event. Within ten months, my cherubic blue-eyed and blond-haired brother was born and became the pride of the family; his Arian features were highly prized. Fourteen months later, I came along, frail by comparison; I was brown-eyed and had an olive complexion like my mother. In addition, I developed typhoid fever and nearly died during my first year. I was clearly not another "golden child," but I would soon make up for it with my wit and clown-like antics.

As my brother and I grew a little older, my mother's attention turned increasingly toward my father, who loved women and drink. In order to represent the family's social position, she was often elegantly dressed and adorned to perfection. Her fresh manicures always matched the Chanel-red of her lipstick. At El Country Club, I would watch her glide into women's circles with poise and precision. From across the room, my father, uncles, and other male associates played billiards, sipped Cuba Libres, and commented on the ladies.

Along with my father's inherited love for whisky, he had the "Scottish Hunter's Clan" inclination for rifles and marksmanship. At the, then exclusive, Sportsmen's Social Club—*El Club de Casa y Tiro*—the trophy shelves were marked by my family's accomplishments. I became a good marksman, which tempered my shameful feeling of being "different"—"Real men could shoot a gun." My skill made my father proud, and he would give me occasional sips of his Cuba Libres: I swallowed these lovingly.

My father always seemed to favor my "golden child" older brother, but fortunately for me, my brother was not interested in hunting or the outdoors, both of which I've always cherished. My brother's lack of interest gave me a unique opportunity to spend prized time with my father. I recall duck hunts involving a small flotilla of twenty-foot dugout longboats with oversized outboard motors. I learned to balance myself precariously in the craft's mid-center directly behind my father while holding a Browning over-and-under 12-gauge shotgun in both arms; both butt and barrels would extend beyond the width of the boat. We would leave before sunrise across the mile-wide Magdalena River toward the wetlands where the marshes meet the Caribbean. Here a phenomenal number of waterfowl would congregate; red and orange tree ducks, *pisingos*, would, at times, obliterate the skies. The longboat captains and their crews maneuvered the narrow passages through the reeds by using long poles, and they collected the shot birds, which seemed to fall like rain. I was fascinated with the boatmen's agility and smooth dark muscular torsos. Even then, I felt an urge to touch them as I would a Greek statue. My long stares would be noticed by my father, who would quickly redirect my attention to the ducks overhead or the crocodiles sunning on a nearby beach. "What is wrong with you?" he would whisper harshly, and then resume shooting. What was wrong with me? I was, once again, puzzled; that shameful, "different" feeling was back. *My imprints were: You are different; there is something intrinsically wrong with you.*

My family also pointed out my "difference" by making fun of my "effeminate mannerisms," such as having both hands on my hips while cocking my head and staring at people demeaningly when I was annoyed. They also did not understand my preference for associating with the "hired help" versus my school friends. I would become enraged when Gustavito would not be allowed to sit at the main dining room table. After all, other children could sit there. Cousins and other "Children of Society" were often specially invited, but I didn't have a particular friendship with them. Worse yet, Gustavito could not attend my own pool birthday parties celebrated at El Country Club. "Who makes up these crazy Son of Society rules?" I would ask furiously. "Don't be so ridiculous," my perplexed mother would say. "It's just the way it is." *My imprints were: I am different; society is unfair; my parents are unfair.*

Another "mind-bending" moment would occur soon after. On a Saturday evening, following one of the many dreaded social events, I was basking in the glory of having just recited an entire, very animated version of a popular children's book, *Rin-Rin the Bullfrog*. I had performed on the terrace above the front lawn, where my mother's father, my adored "Lito," was seated center-stage next to my father and four uncles. They were joyfully applauding and boasting of my actor antics and orator prowess. As they enjoyed their humor and rounds of white rum, I managed to run across the street where Pilar, my dearest classmate, was combing a beautiful doll on her front porch. I took the doll in my lap and proceeded to demonstrate how its hair would look prettier in a pony tail versus "piled-up high." Suddenly, I was startled by my Lito's stern bellow from across the street, "Charles, you come here this instant!" Frightened, I dropped the doll and ran to the now standing group of all-male authority figures. "Boys don't play with dolls," my wide-eyed grandfather stammered. "Are you a *marica* [faggot] or something?" They all glared at me with disgust. I felt terrible but didn't understand why. That night, I overheard my mother saying that having a "faggot son" was one of the worst misfortunes that could befall a mother, and "more painful than the death of one's own child." I could not comprehend the "faggot" concept, but I began to know shame; it felt horribly demeaning. *My imprint was: You should be ashamed because you are different.*

At about this same period in my life, my family's generational alcoholism became undeniably manifest. My father loved women and whisky. He justified his drinking by quoting his Scottish heritage; his womanizing was a good-old Latin tradition. Despite my Lito's numerous interventions and financial bailouts, we remained in fiscal trouble. At night, I remember violent loud arguments that scared me as I hid under the sheets. In the mornings, my mother would sit alone at the dining room table sipping black coffee, her face bruised, vacantly staring across the courtyard at the red acacia tree. Somehow, I felt responsible for her sadness. On my way to school one day, we happened to stop across from a bus stop where, a stranger, an older woman, was crying inconsolably. I didn't know why, but I began to weep; I felt responsible for her sadness too. *My imprint was: You are responsible for others' feelings and emotions.*

One day, after my father returned from a long "business trip," it was announced that we had been granted permanent American resident's visas. We were selling everything and the family was moving from Colombia to California. Gustavito, of course, would not be coming with us, so I was initially devastated. My mother convinced me we would return to visit, and in time, the move to Modesto, California began to sound like a great adventure. Barranquilla and Modesto were Sister Cities I was told; we would learn English, attend college, and become Colombian-Americans! This move would be the first and most dramatic of my family's alcoholic geographical cures, but several others would follow. *My imprints were: Life is unpredictable; change is scary.*

In the winter of 1964, we moved to Modesto, California. Our first home was an old two-bedroom farm cottage in the middle of a large walnut orchard; the nearest paved road was barely visible from the kitchen window. Although we bore Scottish names, we spoke no English. It was all strangely foreign yet nicely new—my father had stopped drinking and so had the late-night angry arguments. My fearful feelings were being replaced by a sense of adventure.

Shortly after our arrival, a bilingual family friend assisted with our school enrollment and helped my parents to find employment. The following Monday morning, I recall my first icy walk to Lincoln Elementary School. It was cold, so my brother and I wore our plaid woolen ponchos; some kids called us "wetbacks," a term I wouldn't come to understand until later; this memory still makes me smile. I remember my parents waving as they passed us on the way to their first American jobs at the Campbell's Soup cannery. Within months, we were becoming fluent in our new language, and soon afterwards, my mother began discussing our future. My brother and I would go to college, and we should become lawyers or doctors; as it turned out, he became a lawyer and I a doctor.

My parents worked long hours of overtime, determined to provide us with "the standards to which we were accustomed." Three years later, my younger brother was born at Doctor's Hospital and we had upgraded to a three-bedroom two-story home on Melrose Avenue. It had its own fenced backyard and a front yard complete with green lawns, elm trees, and paved sidewalks. Our school friends and neighbors joked about our "interesting accents" and commented on how frequently we ate rice, but everyone was friendly enough. Four years after our arrival in Modesto, my father became restless. Despite his hard work, we were not "moving ahead" fast enough; "a new future had to be forged." His drinking resumed as did the late-night arguments. *My imprints were: Life is scary; you can't count on your family.*

Around this time, my father's affluent and known-to-be gay oldest brother offered him a management position in Puerto Rico. Today, I realize this move was another alcoholic geographical cure; we sold most of the household goods, packed, and moved from Modesto to San Juan. Here, my brother and I were enrolled at the Colegio Santa Teresita, a private Catholic school with a long waiting list. My influential uncle had, of course, facilitated an almost-immediate admission. A year later, my father again grew restless. A "promising" opportunity had become available distributing John Deere large-farm equipment along the Caribbean coast. Soon we found ourselves back where we had started, in Barranquilla, Colombia. Here my third and fourth brothers were born. Financially, matters improved considerably but our home life deteriorated due to my father's worsening alcoholism. As I turned thirteen, I was introduced to marijuana, cocaine, and white rum, and instantly, I loved the way they made me feel: confident and powerful.

Concurrently, I also discovered another mind-altering experience: sex with men. Most of my male sexual partners were ten to twenty years my seniors. I found that, when high, I could openly solicit gay sex on certain streets late at night. While intoxicated, I was aggressive and rarely turned down; this experience was empowering in a strange way—it, too, felt like a drug-induced high. Following such encounters, I felt filthy and vowed never to do it again; I would run home to shower and scrub my skin. This cycle kept repeating itself, and I lived in constant fear of being discovered. *My imprint was: You are a shameful person who deserves punishment.*

As I turned fifteen, an opportunity arose for my escape to Modesto, California with the Sister City's student exchange program. This move would be my own first geographical cure. I returned to Modesto to live with a wonderful "All-American" family who embraced and nurtured me. In this new environment, my alcohol, drug, and sex addiction took a reprieve. I completed high school and was accepted to the University of California. As I was finishing my Bachelor of Science, my old "bad habits" resurfaced; another geographical cure was due. I felt the need to move to a land far away where neither my biological or adoptive families could discover my homosexuality and drug use. Not surprisingly, I decided to attend medical school at the University of Minnesota.

It was in Minneapolis, during my first year in medical school, that I met my long-term partner of thirty years, Steven. From the beginning, I have never felt "filthy" about our love, yet I was compelled to keep our live-in relationship a secret for almost a decade. I simply could not risk rejection by my family, an experience some of my friends had known in telling their own families. Even when I graduated from medical school with honors, I prohibited Steven from attending the graduation ceremonies because my family was visiting; he was understandably angry and hurt. That same month, we relocated to Baltimore where I had been accepted into a prestigious OB/GYN residency program. I had always loved women; I've simply never have had a sexual thought about one. Since I delighted in delivering babies, I decided I could best serve mothers and infants as a doctor.

As I was completing my four-year residency program, I began hearing rumors of a "killer gay" virus that was decimating San Francisco and New York. From Colombia, I learned that the "dreaded gay" disease affected a prominent married uncle and my cousin, a distinguished Jesuit priest. Steven and I were both terrified, but we refused to discuss it openly; the HIV virus had just been identified and there was no effective treatment; besides, we were not "sex-club groupies"—we were a couple at "low-risk"; as my coffee cup says, "DENIAL is not a river in EGYPT."

After completing my residency program, Steven and I moved again, this time to North Carolina where I accepted a position as a Research Fellow and as Assistant Professor at Duke University Medical Center. It was in Durham that I met an NBA bound star-athlete who happened to be addicted to cocaine. We became secret lovers. This time, my addictions dragged me into a rapid downward spiral that nearly killed me. Fearing my imminent demise, Steven called my family and identified himself as my gay lover. Together, they planned my intervention, which is how I was directed into treatment and subsequently found myself seated before the North Carolina Medical Board in a high-back leather chair, openly discussing my health status. It was following this fateful meeting that I remained sober and began my healing journey at Pavillon, a then unique pastoral recovery haven, nestled in the blue-green mountains of North Carolina.

In the years to follow, my medical career was transformed; from an Obstetrician Gynecologist, I became an Addictions and HIV Specialist. Spurred by my own afflictions, I became Director of a Chemical Dependency Treatment Center that emphasized the relationship between HIV and Hepatitis C transmission disease progression resulting from drug use. I also established and directed the Southeastern North Carolina Rural HIV Project, which served eleven counties. Later, I was called upon by the North Carolina Division of Prisons to become its first Director of HIV Clinical Services. I subsequently brought my acquired skills and knowledge to Oakland, California where I opened a private HIV and Addictions practice. I've lectured widely and carried my message of hope and recovery from community churches to professional organizations. Throughout my endeavors, my heart has continuously and ardently sought to reach out to my patients and audiences, in part because I've had first-hand experience with disease-related societal rejections, disease manifestations, and unpleasant treatments' side effects. Like many others, I too had prepared for death upon my diagnosis, but now, twenty-plus years later, I prepare myself for life on a daily basis. I am conscious of my imprints and I address them as they arise. Three decades of my partner Steven's constant love and companionship have been an absolute blessing. My family and I have become closer than ever; they've remained at my side through it all. My life has become a magnificent journey, and today, it's far from over.

Freedom from Dysfunctional Beliefs to Be My Authentic Self (Vic Feazell)

In the mid-1990s, I had everything a man could possibly want in order to be happy. I had a nine thousand square foot mansion on three gated and manicured acres in Austin, Texas, and it was paid for. I had a few million dollars in the bank, and I drove a brand new, paid for, Mercedes. I had a beautiful wife, a handsome ten year old son, and I even had a couple of girlfriends I kept on the side. Even better, I had all the time in the world to do whatever I wanted, whenever I wanted, because I had already retired from my law practice a few years earlier at the ripe old age of age of forty. I had the best of everything money could buy, first class all the way, but I was miserable and I didn't know why.

By the time I found my way to Pavillon and met Liliane and Gilles, my wife had already found out about one of my girlfriends, thrown me out of the house, and instituted divorce proceedings, but she couldn't make up her mind whether or not to go through with it. I couldn't decide whether to try to get back with my wife, to live with the girlfriend she had caught me with, or whether to do something else entirely. When I was at one place, I wanted to be at the other. When I was at the other, I wanted to be somewhere else. I had acute option anxiety. I wanted it all, but I wasn't happy with any of it. I was making everyone miserable, including myself. My son hated me and didn't want anything to do with me anymore, and I didn't blame him. I was a selfish, temperamental bastard. My life was unmanageable, and I had no idea how to fix it.

I had been raised the son of a poor, self-educated, rural Baptist preacher in the 1950s and '60s. My family's life was hard, or at least we were convinced it was. We moved about every year and a half from one small church field to the next on the promise that the new congregation, unlike the last, would pay my dad a livable wage every week. But then, after awhile, the church members would somehow fail to make the payments. Then they would figure out a way to blame their failure on the preacher, or to find something else wrong with him, so they wouldn't have to feel guilty about not living up to their commitments, or at least that's how it seemed to me. I was about twelve when I started noticing that my dad never stood up for himself. I believed he was weak. I promised myself I would never be that way; that I would always stand up for myself... and for other people. I began to develop a deep hatred for injustice and for powerful people who took advantage of the weak.

One year when I was in junior high school, my younger sister and I were pulled out of class two weeks before Christmas because my dad had just been fired by a majority vote of the church elders. We were told to vacate the parsonage immediately because the new preacher and his family needed to move in. I can still recall the sound of the ice cracking under the weight of the U-Haul trailer tires as we slowly pulled out of the frozen, gravel driveway, dragging all of our possessions behind us, and taking one last glance back at what had been our home. We felt uncertainty and fear from not knowing where we would go. I remember the defeated look on my dad's face and the scorn and anger in my mother's tortured voice as she cried out and asked, "What now, God? We're homeless!" It was the first time I had heard that word..."homeless." The sound of it resonated in my soul and I vowed when I was an adult that this same situation would never happen to me.

I remember that Mom and Dad took turns driving our old car nonstop the thousand plus miles to my grandmother's house, our last resort. We ate bologna sandwiches in the car, used the restroom in roadside parks, and prayed we wouldn't run out of gas money or break down before we got there. When we surprised grandmother with a late night knock on her door, she reluctantly took us in. For years when I would remember that night and its feeling of helpless desperation, I would get angry, sometimes at God, sometimes at Christians, sometimes at my mom and dad, but most often at myself, and then I would get depressed and irritable.

My mother loved us, but she was an angry woman. She felt she deserved better out of life, and no matter how much she tried, how much she prayed, or how much she disciplined her children, it was never enough. My sister and I would cower, fearful of being beaten yet again, while being forced to listen, day in and day out, to her hysterical raging. She thought my dad was a dismal failure, and she was quick to tell him so, again and again. She criticized his use of the English language. She criticized the way he smiled. She even criticized the way he walked. My sister and I did not escape her venom either. Nothing we did was ever good enough. She would make us feel guilty for being born. We were told often, in hysterical and excruciating detail, about how much pain she suffered giving birth to us, how much she cried, how much she bled, what it looked like, and how unworthy we all were of her love. I grew up with deep feelings of inadequacy, guilt, and shame that weighed upon me, constantly affecting my self-esteem and my relationships with other people, and I didn't even know it.

After awhile, my dad found another church and we were pulling the U-Haul trailer to another dingy little parsonage. Dad worked hard and was successful at this new church. He cared for it like a gardener diligently tending his plants. New members joined, people tithed, and a building fund was established for the new and bigger sanctuary we would soon need. The church grew in number and everything seemed great. Dad got his first new car; mom had a refrigerator that worked, and for the first time in our lives, my sister and I wore clothes that were not hand-me-downs.

Then, after a couple of years, rumors of dissatisfaction began to surface. Talk increased among some of the members about how, since the church was bigger now, it deserved to have a better preacher, a preacher with a seminary degree, a preacher who knew how to use proper grammar from the pulpit. Within another year, Mom and Dad were moving again. I had managed by then to graduate from high school a year early. I found a job, moved out on my own, and was looking into ways to attend college. My fifteen year old sister wasn't as fortunate. In order to get away from Mom and Dad and to avoid another trip with the U-Haul, she married the first boy she dated. He was a recent Viet Nam veteran with a drinking problem who brought the horrors of the war back home with him; on a regular basis, he took his anger out on my sister with his fists until she became a physically and emotionally battered, seventeen year old divorcee with a new baby in tow.

I eventually got into college, taking a full course load and holding down three jobs at the same time because I had to pay my own way. Sometimes the stress was almost more than I could handle. That was when I first began to experience panic attacks. I paid my own tuition and living expenses and sent money to Mom and Dad whenever I could. I was determined to pull myself out from the poverty in which I had grown up. I was driven by the insecurity and fear of never having enough. At age twenty, I found myself in the emergency room thinking I was having a heart attack. The doctor explained that it was not my heart, but a panic attack; he recommended that I reduce my course load and quit one of my jobs. The next day, I went back to school with my full course load, gutted up, and I kept working my three jobs. When I would feel a panic attack coming on, I would internalize it, press it down, and shame myself for being weak...like my dad.

Right before college graduation, I decided to apply to law school. I wanted to get rich, and I had already figured out that I wasn't good enough at sports and my fledgling music career was going nowhere. I had thought about being a preacher and had pastored two small churches while in college. I was fully and officially ordained as a Baptist minister by the time I was only nineteen. But I knew that the pastorate was no way for me to get rich, and I had already encountered some of the petty church politics I had witnessed my dad experience, so I decided during my senior year that the law was the way to go. An established older minister in our town heard that I was applying to law school rather than going to the seminary so he paid a surprise visit to my home. He told me that I had "baked the cake," but I was now "refusing to put icing on it" by not going on to the seminary. He was very concerned and he seemed sincere when he warned me that law school would surely be my path to hell. Since he had never been around before when I really needed help, I thanked him for his concern and showed him the door.

I couldn't afford to move so I applied to only one law school, the closest, Baylor. I had been told that Baylor was hard to get into and that I would probably have to apply several times before I got admitted. I had planned to work for a year or two after college graduation and save up some money before beginning law school, but Baylor accepted me on my first try. I was told not to turn down the school or I'd probably never be accepted again. So two months after receiving my bachelor's degree, I was sitting in class at Baylor School of Law, flat broke and wondering how I would pay for my next set of classes. But I found a job and found a way.

Occasionally, I would have to drop out for a semester or two in order to work and save for tuition. The dean of the law school was an understanding and sympathetic man who was very accommodating of my unusual schedule. I now jokingly say that I crammed three years of law school into only seven short years.

After graduating from Baylor Law School, I was exhausted and in debt to my eyeballs. I didn't want to take a job carrying someone else's briefcase, and I didn't want to work for one of the large insurance defense firms, so I set out on my own and paid a couple of Waco lawyers to let me use one end of their library table to meet with my occasional clients. The rest I did out of the trunk of my car. The Monday after I graduated, I went to the courthouse, found a district judge, showed him my bar exam scores, and got him to give me the oath and swear me in. Then I asked him to appoint me to an indigent criminal case so I could get to work...and get paid. He was reluctant to appoint a brand new lawyer to handle a criminal case alone, but once I talked him into it, he set us for jury trial ten days later. I tried my first jury trial ten days out of law school, an assault on a police officer case, and won it. The judge was so impressed that he paid me double what he usually paid for court-appointed cases. My reputation began to grow as I was appointed to more cases and won them all, one after another. I also started handling civil cases and quickly gained a reputation as a fighter and a crusader for justice. If there were a battle to fight, an injustice to be corrected, or someone who needed a champion to stand up for him, I was the man, regardless of the consequences, and I didn't care who I made mad in the process.

After about a year of trying criminal cases back to back, I was court-appointed to a case that had been assigned to the First Assistant District Attorney. I had never met him before. He was a big shot in my mind. I called and made an appointment to talk with him about the case. I arrived at the appointed time and his secretary greeted me and asked me to have a seat in the lobby. I waited for an hour, then another hour, all along being told by his secretary that he would be with me shortly. After another hour, he came walking through the lobby with another man and walked right past me toward the exit. "Sir," I said, as he passed by, "we have an appointment to talk about a case." He spun on his heels, gave me an angry look, and began loudly to berate me in front of everyone present. He said, "I know why you are here...and if you're representing him then you're just as bad as he is." He called me a few choice names and when his angry face got right into mine, I could smell the strong odor of alcohol on his breath.

The humiliation I experienced reminded me of things I had seen my dad have to put up with at the hands of people who thought they were better than him. It pulled up all kinds of childhood memories. My anger flared—that was the instant I decided to go into politics. "You know what," I said, as he was walking out the door, "I'm going to run against your boss and when I win, I'm going to fire you!" He laughed as the door closed behind him.

A year later, after the votes were counted, I had beaten the entrenched, establishment-supported, incumbent District Attorney in an upset victory and found myself in the position of chief law enforcement officer of Waco/McLennan County, supervising a dozen attorneys and that many more support staff. I had never even had my own secretary and had only two and a half years of law practice under my belt. I attacked the job with all my might, working long days and long nights. Within a year, my office had the highest felony conviction rate in the State of Texas. I soon gained the reputation of being a fearless champion in the courtroom, trying most of the lengthy and difficult cases myself. We were an exemplary office, but my home life was already suffering. My young son seldom saw me, and my wife was finding other things to keep her busy and not all of it was good.

I always figured there would be time for family after I got a few more things accomplished. I already had my eye on the attorney general's office, maybe even governor. And then I could write my own ticket. Some firm would pay me big money just to have my name on its letterhead. Everything was working out. I was becoming somebody...somebody who would never have to leave anywhere in disgrace.

Then I got a call from the Texas Rangers. They had arrested a mass murderer, a drifter named Henry Lee Lucas, who, they claimed, had committed three murders in my county. He had confessed to them and they wanted to bring him to Waco to plead guilty so they could close the cases and get them off their books. "It will be a good photo-op," they told me. "Plead him guilty, get on TV, and we'll be on our way." Henry Lucas had already confessed to over three hundred murders across the country, and I had already seen more than a few law enforcement officials on TV getting their face time with this modern day boogie man. Now it was my turn for some favorable publicity standing in front of the cameras flanked by Texas Rangers and their version of Hannibal Lecter. But there was one problem. I didn't think Lucas had committed the crimes.

We already had a good suspect for one of the murders and the suspect had recently been convicted by a jury for a murder almost identical to the one the Rangers were saying Lucas had done. But if Lucas had not done the crimes, how was it that he was able to confess to them in such detail? I read and re-read the confessions, but they didn't ring true. The Rangers said, "He told us things only the true killer could know," but in reviewing the files, I realized that Lucas's confessions didn't say anything more than anyone could have said who had seen the crime scene photos. Our initial, cursory investigation revealed to us that Lucas had actually been thousands of miles away from some of the murder scenes at the time the murders were committed. I asked myself why the Rangers had not been able to discover what we had found in just a few short weeks of looking. The Rangers continued to press me to bring Lucas to Waco and let him plead guilty, but instead, I called together a Grand Jury to investigate how it was that Lucas had confessed to these murders that we had good reason to believe he had not committed.

That is when my life went off track like a runaway train without a driver. The head of the Texas Rangers at that time had formerly been the deputy director of the FBI under J. Edgar Hoover, and he had learned a lot of dirty tricks by studying at Hoover's feet. He considered my investigation an insult to the Rangers and a personal attack against him. "If you are attacking the Rangers, you are attacking America," he told me. I remember the day I visited with him in his office and shared the results of our initial investigation. I had naively thought that he would welcome the information and clean up his own backyard. But he was not interested. He told me he did not intend to reopen a single Lucas case, not even the one I showed him where Lucas had been in jail in north Texas when the murder was being committed in southern Louisiana. Instead, he pointed his finger in my face and told me he was opening an investigation of me and that the Rangers and the FBI were going to work full-time until they found something. "If we want you, we'll get you," he said. He told me what other law enforcement professionals had told me over the past several weeks—that I had violated the law enforcement brotherhood. "Right or wrong," I had been told, "we stick together." Suddenly, I found myself an outcast in the law enforcement community that, only weeks before, had welcomed me with awards, resolutions, and open arms.

I didn't back down. To me, this man was just another petty tyrant, like the church deacons my dad had dealt with, threatening my freedom and my livelihood because I was trying to do what was right. I went ahead and called together the Grand Jury and started taking testimony from witnesses across the country, including the Texas Rangers who had taken the confessions from Lucas. One of the Rangers, before he went in to testify, stuck his big, ham of a hand in my face, touched my nose with his finger, and said, "Mark my word; you will live to regret the day you ever heard the name Henry Lee Lucas."

After a series of legal battles, we got custody of Lucas himself and he became our star witness. As it turned out, the Rangers had kept Lucas on Thorazine, an antipsychotic drug that makes people pliable and subject to suggestion. Our expert doctor told the Grand Jury that Lucas had been on enough Thorazine to "knock out a horse." Then they would let him look at crime scene photographs so eventually he would "confess." Agencies from across the country started re-opening Lucas cases when they heard about our investigation. The Rangers had egg on their faces. They were embarrassed and they were mad.

Throughout our Grand Jury investigation, there were rumors that I would be indicted by a Federal Grand Jury sitting in Austin or San Antonio. Every week, there was a new set of rumors. Then people I knew started getting Federal subpoenas handed to them by intimidating looking men wearing bland suits and Government Issue sunglasses. My accountant was subpoenaed. The lady who owned the Chinese restaurant where I would eat occasionally got subpoenaed. Attorneys I knew were subpoenaed. My barber was subpoenaed. They were all told, "Make it easy on yourself. Tell us something on Vic Feazell."

Then a TV reporter with Belo Broadcasting Corporation in Dallas began a series of "investigative reports" about me. The TV station ran eleven different episodes in each newscast on three television stations across the state, spread out over a three month period. Each "investigative report" accused me of a different crime or dereliction of duty. I was accused of taking bribes. I was accused of being in cahoots with drug dealers. I was accused of not prosecuting people who had assaulted policemen. The rest of the media went crazy and a feeding frenzy ensued. I was followed and hounded by reporters night and day. By the time I could prove that what one Dallas reporter said about me on TV was a lie, three more lies were circulating. My explanation, my evidence, was old news. The new news was the latest allegation.

The head of the Texas Rangers held a news conference in which he said it was obvious I had made false allegations against the Texas Rangers in order to deflect attention from my own wrongdoings. "It was a smoke screen," he said, "because Feazell knew we were coming after him long before he got involved in the Lucas matter." While watching the news that night, my jaw dropped open when I heard his words. The memory was still fresh in my mind of him telling me he wasn't going to investigate the Lucas confessions, but he was going to investigate me.

From that moment, and for the next seven years, I fought, even in my sleep, for my very survival. It would take me page upon page even to scratch the surface of everything that happened during those years. I became a man driven, driven by the necessity of fighting for my freedom, my reputation, and my life. My wife and I tried the best we could to keep what was going on from our son, but children are perceptive even at age three. One day, I was driving him to his kindergarten class at the Montessori School. He was strapped in his car seat as usual, but he wasn't his usual talkative self. I was preoccupied, trying to figure out every move and counter-move, and which shoe would drop next. Then I realized we were almost to the school and he hadn't said anything for the entire drive. When I looked at him, his little lip was puckered and he had a tear in his eye. When I asked, "What's wrong, buddy?" he answered in the saddest little voice, "I don't want you to go to jail, Daddy." I cried. I couldn't help myself.

The judge in charge of renewing the term of the Grand Jury that was investigating the Lucas confessions saw very plainly what was happening to me. I had become the poster child, the living example, of what would happen to you if you violated the law enforcement brotherhood. When the Grand Jury expired, we still had several witnesses to hear from and several more cases and confessions to examine. I believe that if the Grand Jury had been extended, there would have been indictments handed down on two Texas Rangers. The judge refused the Grand Jury's request for an extension of time, and its time expired before having an opportunity to vote.

Lucas was returned to prison on death row in Huntsville to serve his several life sentences and to await execution on a case called Orange Socks that he had confessed to after having seen the photographs. Documents later proved that Lucas was in Florida at the time of that murder, selling scrap metal and cashing a check. Orange Socks was the only death penalty case that then Governor George Bush ever commuted to life. By the time, the Grand Jury disbanded and Lucas was back in prison; I was involved in a heated reelection campaign.

Six weeks before the election, I was indicted, arrested, handcuffed, and marched through the streets on live television. Belo Broadcasting from Dallas had four cameras there so it would be sure to have all the live action when it broke into the soap operas to show me being arrested. At the same time, my wife and son were removed by several FBI agents from a restaurant where they were having breakfast and brought back to our house where they were forced to sit on the couch and watch ten to fifteen men with badges and guns ransack our home, take everything out of every drawer and cabinet, empty out the cereal boxes, open the meat in the freezer, dig up the flowerbeds, take the mattresses off the bed, go through my son's toys, and rake the insulation in the attic. They searched the empty dog house in the backyard—empty because six months earlier, they had killed our dog because he barked at the men who were illegally tapping our phone from the pole behind our house.

My wife asked the FBI whether she could turn on the television so our son would not have to watch them searching our things. When she turned it on, the programming was immediately interrupted by a news bulletin showing me being led up the sidewalk in front of the courthouse in handcuffs. When I saw the cameras, I raised my thumbs in a defiant thumbs up gesture and said, "I think you know what's going on here...what I've said all along, and I'll still be proven right." The sight of seeing his dad on TV in handcuffs traumatized my son for years.

I refused to try to raise bond and went on a publicized hunger strike that lasted less than four hours before they let me out on my personal recognizance. Two weeks before the election, they released the search warrant affidavit and inventory, and they hand delivered it to all the news outlets. My phone started ringing off the wall. The inventory said that they had taken "drug paraphernalia" from our home. It took a while to figure out what the FBI was calling drug paraphernalia. They had taken a toy syringe from my son's play doctor kit. But by the time I could answer the questions, they were off on the next allegation. The federal prosecutor, who was friends with the head of the Texas Rangers, told a local news reporter that I would be enjoying the snows of Leavenworth by Christmas. I wanted to cry, but I gutted up.

Election night was tense. If I lost, I would still be facing a criminal trial later that year, and I would have no way to make a living in the interim. At least if I won the election, I would still have my job...and a forum from which to speak to the public. If I lost my job, I lost my home. And I didn't even have a place where I could pull a U-Haul trailer. Grandma was dead and I wasn't even allowed to leave the county. It seemed I was worse off than my dad had ever been.

By eleven-thirty that night, I had won the election, but it was only the primary election. I still had the general election to go through and I had another opponent waiting in the wings to take me out in November. The Texas Rangers had made sure I was opposed in both elections. The next day I started work on that, and I continued to run the DA's office and try cases so my work wouldn't become an issue.

The second election was dirtier than the first. I was accused of being un-American and of being against law enforcement, although I still had the highest felony conviction in Texas. And I was accused of taking bribes. The FBI had found two old criminal defense lawyers who had never deposited any cash in their business account in all the years they had been in practice together, which is impossible for a criminal defense lawyer to do...legally anyway. The government made a tax case against them and then offered them criminal and civil immunity if they would say they had given part of the money to me to dismiss cases for them.

I won the general election as well. The margin was not as big. It took until after two in the morning for all the votes to be counted. I was afraid for a while that night that the lies had been believed. I had to win every battle. There was no choice. One misstep could have landed me in prison for the rest of my life.

After I won the primary election, the government got a change of venue from Waco to Austin, saying it couldn't get a fair trial in Waco. The real reason was the FBI wanted the tactical advantage of making me put on a defense away from home, thus costing me more money—money I did not have. In addition to trying to lock me away for eighty years, it also filed a motion to take away my home and to forfeit it to the government as ill gotten gain once I was found guilty and hauled off to Leavenworth in leg irons. My wife was a stay at home mom. My son had just turned four. The prospect of leaving them without a breadwinner and without a home weighed on me more than the idea of growing old in prison. With tears in my eyes, I asked my wife to divorce me if I were found guilty.

The day after our late night general election victory, I had to drive to Austin, ninety miles away, to be in court at eight in the morning for pre-trial hearings on my case, The United States of America versus Victor Fred Feazell. I was so tired when I stood as my case was called out by the court clerk. I remember thinking, "The United States of America...Are all fifty of them against me?" Thank God for my lawyer, Gary Richardson, who was there and stood with me. Gary was my friend. He was ten years my senior and we had worked on several lawsuits together before I became DA and he became the United States Attorney for the Eastern District of Oklahoma. He had been my mentor. Gary had just left the U.S. Attorney's Office a couple of months before I was arrested. His number was the one I dialed when I was given my "one phone call" after I was arrested.

We went to trial almost a year after I was arrested. The trial lasted six exhausting and terrifying weeks as witness after witness got on the stand, but none of them connected me to any illegal money or wrongdoing. By then, only one of the old lawyers who had made a deal to testify for the government was willing to say he had given me a bribe. He recalled giving it to me on a certain day in his office. However, official court records we presented to the jury proved that I was in court in another town a hundred miles away trying a change of venue murder case and that I had been there three weeks prior and was three weeks after.

The jury found me not guilty on its first vote and several of the jurors held a press conference afterward saying it was obvious to them that the government had tried to frame me. The next day, I was back in Waco working on a murder case where a stepfather had burned his two stepsons to death in a shed in their backyard. I had promised the boys' mother I would personally try the case.

Three months after the jury had returned a guilty verdict against the man, I resigned from my job as DA and opened my own little office across the street so I could pursue a lawsuit I had filed against the Belo Broadcasting Corporation, the television station that had run the libelous news stories against me. Gary Richardson and I took the depositions and prepared for trial. I did all of the briefing and legal arguments to the court and Gary presented all the evidence to the jury. After a six week trial, the jury returned the largest libel verdict in United States history: $58 million. Not only had I been found not guilty in Austin of all the charges against me, where the government had the burden of proof, but I had taken on the burden of proof myself and proved that each and every thing the government had said about me was false, and that it had been said with malice. I stood up in court and thanked the jury on the record. I said, "I want to thank twenty-four very important people; the twelve in Austin who found me not guilty and the twelve of you today who have found me innocent."

During all that time, I had managed to keep my faith. Faith in God that He would deliver me was often the only thing that kept me able to put one foot in front of the other. I would get up before the sun rose every morning and read the Psalms and meditate on how God had delivered David, and I would pray. And I would ask God to deliver me. And I would thank God for already delivering me. I knew that fear was my worst enemy, so I would ask God to help me live in Faith and to keep me from fear.

Back when I was seventeen or eighteen years old, I had come across a little twenty-two page book on Faith by an elderly Pentecostal preacher in Oklahoma who had learned the lessons of Faith at a very early age and was miraculously healed of a deadly childhood disease. Over the next couple of decades, I read and re-read that little book. I'm so glad I did because it prepared me to survive what I would have to go through later on. I remember my favorite quote: "When fear comes in the front door, Faith runs out the back. But when Faith comes in the front door, fear runs out the back. The choice is yours. Who are you going to let in?"

That lesson helped me understand that it really was my choice whether I lived in Faith or in fear. Many times fear would sneak into my consciousness for a day or two, or a week, but when I realized it was there, I would invite Faith back in...and

Faith would always respond. I am not saying it was easy, because it certainly was not. What I am saying is that Faith works and it worked for me.

We mediated the Belo case a few weeks after the verdict and a settlement was reached for a cash payment just a few days before the appeal bond was due. We did not get the full $58 million, but we did get a lot. Suddenly the pressure was off, so I thought. I was a free man and was debt-free for the first time in my life.

The following week, word started to leak out that we had settled the case. My phone rang constantly. Relatives I had never heard of, relatives I had heard of, people who had helped me campaign for office, and even a couple of old high school acquaintances contacted me asking for money. I said "no" a lot, but I said yes a lot too. Before I realized it, I had given away several hundred thousand dollars. My doorbell started ringing at six in the morning. One morning I didn't answer it. I just let it ring. A man climbed over our back fence and put his face to the window to see whether we were at home. We eventually had to tape butcher paper over our windows for privacy. Two weeks later, I moved my family to an apartment in Austin while we looked for a new home. I drove back and forth from Waco to Austin every day for a couple months to wind down my law practice. I had planned to reopen in Austin and continue working. I moved all of my files to a storage unit in Austin, and I moved my secretary to Austin to start organizing the office. During that time, Gary and I tried another jury trial against a natural gas company whose negligence had caused an explosion resulting in a man losing all of his fingers. It was a hard fought trial. The FBI and the ATF were involved in that case because they were accusing our client of arson. We won the case, made ourselves and our client a lot of money, and made the government even madder.

Then one morning, I received a panicked call from my secretary's husband. The FBI had just been at their new apartment, arrested her, and taken her away in handcuffs. The charge, I finally discovered, was that she was considered a material witness in a new investigation the FBI had launched against me. They claimed that by moving to Austin, she was a fugitive trying to flee. The ride back to Waco in the backseat of the FBI car was so stressful for her that by the time she arrived at the jail, she had ruptured something in her intestines and had to be hospitalized. They placed armed guards at her hospital door and had the federal judge in Waco appoint one of their friends to be her lawyer. He allowed the Feds to question her while under sedation, and she signed a statement incriminating herself and me in something we had not done. It reminded me of the Thorazine-influenced questioning they had done on Henry Lee Lucas.

The next day, I went to the storage facility with my son to pull some documents for her and my defense. When we arrived, the attendant ran out to meet us and excitedly told us that the FBI had just left and they had told him not to call me. All of my files had been ransacked and a search warrant, signed by the Waco judge, was left lying on the floor. I remember the fear that shot through me like an electrical current. I couldn't believe it was happening again. I remember the look of fright on my little boy's face.

For the next two years, I managed to keep my faith and I fought that case all the way to the Fifth Circuit Court of Appeals in New Orleans and won. The FBI was forced to shut down its investigation. My secretary was released from the hospital after a couple of weeks and moved back to Oklahoma. I decided to close my office and retire from law practice. It was not safe for me to stay in business.

To say I was suffering from post-traumatic stress disorder at that point in my life would be an understatement. I lived in a swirling emotional cocktail of fear, anger, hate, resentment, and a desire for revenge. I would fantasize at night when I was unable to sleep, which was often, about getting even with the people who had tried to take me from my family and lock me up for the rest of my life. I dreamed of the day anarchy would break out so I could find each of them and end their lives.

I started drinking, which was something I had never done before. And I bought the best and strongest marijuana that could be found and I smoked it all day long every day. I went on shopping binges and bought things that I never took out of the package. I started taking Ecstasy on a regular basis. I gave away money left and right and invested in foolish business deals. I stopped communicating with my wife, who was suffering as much as I was, but we never talked about it. I started being unfaithful, paying rent and living expenses for women who would have me over for sex or who would travel out of town with me. I was self-medicating in almost every way I could.

When my wife found out about one of the women, she threw me out of the house, changed the locks, and started turning my son against me. The women I played around with were not sweethearts. One in particular made my life miserable, but I was addicted to the sex and to the verbal abuse. Sometimes I was so emotionally and spiritually disoriented that I would end up sleeping in my car, living like a homeless man in a brand new Mercedes.

Then one day, I got a call from the receptionist at a law office downtown. I had parked my office furniture in one of the law office's spare rooms in return for having my name on the door. She told me that a man had been by there looking for me...twice. She said the second time he was there she saw a pistol in his belt. He didn't leave his name, but he told her I had been to bed with his wife and that he wanted to "talk" with me about it. He told her that he would find me. I had no idea who he was, but I had no reason to doubt what he said. A lot of my recent history I simply did not remember. Needless to say, I didn't want to meet him.

My mind suddenly flashed back to a concerned friend who had recently told me about a place in Canada called Pavillon where people could go for a month and work on their problems in a secure, private setting with no phone, no newspapers, and no visitors. That sounded like just the place for me right then, a place to hide, so I started making calls. I had no idea that Divine Order was at work in my life. I found out that the Pavillon was no longer in Canada and was in the process of relocating to North Carolina. It was about to start its first twenty-eight day session in the U.S. at temporary quarters in the northern part of South Carolina at a place called Look Up Lodge, an old motel in the mountains that had been converted into a church camp of sorts. The person on the phone told me that the session was starting the very next day and it was full, but they had just received a cancellation. I read off my credit card number to the lady, paid for the session, drove to the airport, and caught the next plane I could get on.

I got to Pavillon in time for the opening session called the "hot seat" where all the attendees took turns sitting in the designated chair, introduced themselves, and told why they were there. There were drug addicts, alcoholics, sex addicts, businessmen with cocaine problems, an old man with a history of child sexual abuse, and two young women with anorexia. I felt out of place. When my turn came, I took the chair and told the group that I didn't really have any problems like them. I was just there hiding out from a jealous husband. "I have everything I want and need. I just need a place to hide out and rest a bit." That was the first time I met Liliane and Gilles.

Gilles laughed and said, "We'll get there." He thought it was really funny when I said I didn't have any problems. Liliane smiled at me with that look of total love, understanding, and acceptance that she does so well…and I was hooked. Over the next twenty-eight days, I gradually bared my soul, and the enormity of my experiences over the past decade began to rush over me like a tsunami. I got in touch with parts of myself I had been repressing since childhood, parts I did not want to confront. Gilles would prod me. Liliane would console me.

We learned the Twelve Steps and what they mean. I learned what it is to "practice the Presence of the Higher Power." I learned about trust and I learned new lessons about Faith. I learned about childhood imprints and the powerful and most often negative impact they exert on a person's life. And I started learning how to free myself from my negative childhood imprints.

Going into the last week of the session, we were assigned to break-out groups. I was in a small group being led by Liliane when she looked at me sympathetically and asked, "Vic, why is it you are always bringing women into your life who are exactly like your mother?" I was floored because she was right. That was exactly what I had been doing. Every girlfriend I had ever had, my wife, even my employees I chose mirrored my mother's behavior, temperament, and emotional needs. They had the same expectations; I had to fulfill their every emotional and physical need or else it meant I didn't love them. I had also picked up my mother's imprint that "No matter what I do, it is never good enough."

Through the work we did, I also came to realize why I had the need to try to correct every injustice I saw, even if it meant sacrificing myself; that need stemmed from my childhood imprints as well. Witnessing my dad being disrespected, taken advantage of and mistreated by sanctimonious, religious people had given me a

Jesus complex. I had the compulsion to rush in without thinking, even without being invited, and run the risk of harming myself and making the situation worse.

When I left Pavillon and returned to Austin, I was by no means a cured and enlightened person. I still had problems. I still had a divorce pending. I still had enemies in high places. But I had the tools for working on myself. I realized that I am a work in progress, and God is not through with me yet, if I will let Him have His way. Part of the trick to letting God have His way in your life is learning to set your ego aside and relate to yourself and others with the Spiritual Self, which is your Wonder Child.

I also learned the value and necessity of forgiveness. Forgiveness, I learned, is for my own benefit more than for the benefit of the person I am forgiving. It frees and releases you so that your spiritual energy can be directed into positive living. God settles all scores: I don't have to. I had been home for a few months when I woke up in the middle of the night in a cold sweat and knew what I had to do. I got on my knees next to my bed and began to pray. I called to mind the faces of everyone who had tried to put me in prison, the people who had testified against me, and the people who had done angry and hurtful things to me and my family…and I forgave them one by one, calling them by name. I cried and I trembled and when I was finished, I started again. I forgave my mother, and my dad, and the people from my childhood whose names I could not even remember. I even forgave myself. When I finally pulled myself up off the floor, I was a new man.

I learned that we do not live in a Universe of lack, but a Universe of plenty. God is the source of my supply and with Him all things are possible. I learned to pray for my enemies and to ask for blessings upon them, for in doing so, I am bringing blessings upon myself. After a while I learned that I have no enemies. We are all God's children doing the best we can.

In the months and years after going to Pavillon simply to hide, I actually found myself. The divorce was finalized and my ex-wife and I went our separate ways, although we still keep up with each other and at my beckoning she attended the Four Day Workshop that Gilles and Liliane conducted from their home in Lakeway, Texas, since they retired and moved to Austin. My ex-wife is now putting her life and soul in order using the same tools I learned to use at Pavillon. My son is grown now and he is attending the Four Day Session as I write this. There are no more FBI investigations of me. Most of the powerful people I made angry have since died or retired or mellowed and grown in Spirit like I have. The IRS changed a tax law, made it retroactive, and audited me. I ended up giving most of the money I still had to the government to settle my tax bill. Oh well, I know the source of my supply and God has already begun replacing as much of it as I need. I started practicing law again and now have successful offices in Waco and in Austin, and I have the best employees I have ever had.

I met a wonderful woman. At first I wasn't attracted to her, in spite of her beauty, poise, and calm nature. Then I realized it was because she wasn't anything at all like my mother. Liliane's words echoed in my brain. She was right; I didn't want another woman like my mother in my life. I didn't need the trauma drama. Cecelia and I were married in Maui on Valentine's Day in the year 2000. We are about to celebrate our eleventh anniversary. I have never been more at peace or more happy.

I still have a way to go. Like I said, our lives are a work in progress. But one thing I do know: I am a good person today. And I will remain a good person because I have the tools to work with.

When Liliane told me she was writing a book, I could hardly wait to read it. I knew from my previous experiences with her that it would be a treasure chest of Spiritual Knowledge, Insight, and Love. I was right. I am already on my third reading. It brings to mind the lessons and insight wisdom I gained during my twenty-eight days at Pavillon. It is a concise, yet complete manual for transformation away from negative childhood imprints and core addictions into the freedom and joy of living in Spirit. Another thing that moved me about the book is Liliane's willing vulnerability as she bared her own soul to reveal her childhood experiences and the imprints that brought her through the valley of her own shadow of death to the bright and sunny mountaintop of the enlightened experience. Liliane and Gilles are truly enlightened masters whose very presence in the room can raise a person's consciousness.

I encourage you to keep reading this book again and again and to be Blessed. I have. And while you are reading it, know that I am probably reading it again along with you. After all, we are a work in progress.

Over the years, through study, meditation, and my experiences with Gilles and Liliane, I gradually learned that a person's life history is basically a reflection of his or her belief about God. As my beliefs about God gradually changed from that of a punitive, vindictive, and fickle God to a caring, Loving God, my life began to change, and consequently, I began writing a new life history, fully incorporating and accepting my past, but moving forward in a new and better direction. I began to realize that the beliefs and ideas I accepted about God and about myself would be expressed, out-pictured, in my life, in my surroundings, and in all my relationships. When I began truly to believe that my happiness is important to God, I began to find true Joy in my life, and I started learning how to keep it, by practicing the Presence of God.

Thank you, Liliane.

Freedom from Religious, Sexual, & Economic Imprints (Gilles Desjardins)

I was born in Montreal in a Catholic, French Canadian family. My parents were poor. My mother's father was a mean alcoholic who died of alcoholism. My father came from an alcoholic family, and he was a "functional alcoholic." What I mean by functional is that my father went to work every day, but went to bed drunk, every night. He never owned a house or a car. We never went on vacations, and he did not have a bank account.

My parents inherited imprints from their families of not being worthy, not being good enough, and not having any rights to success. They never had a chance at a better life. They never got help or treatment for their issues as adult children of alcoholics; such treatments did not even exist in their time. Neither was my father's alcoholism ever addressed. My parents were two beautiful souls imprisoned in a world of dysfunction and addictions. They were casualties of the religious and socio-economic structures of their time. Born into fear, they died fearful. Some of the most prevalent familial, cultural, and religious imprints I received in my childhood were:

- *We are French Canadians so we have no power; we are not good enough.*
- *English speaking people are smarter and superior to us so they have the power.*
- *We are made for a small life/poor life, so don't aim higher…be happy to have a steady job; don't rock the boat.*
- *We are poor; there is not enough money or opportunities; money is for the rich and powerful.*
- *Politicians are dirty and corrupt; don't trust them.*
- *The church and the priest are God; they are always right. You must fear God.*
- *Sex is a sin; it's dirty and not to be talked about.*
- *Marriage is a prison, a struggle, a burden, and it is forever.*

For Father, Love was:	Providing for the family Not having problems Not having debts
For Mother, Love was:	Cleaning Cooking Criticizing Pointing out what was wrong with everyone
For Father, Happiness was:	Having a steady job Being free of debt Medicating feelings with alcohol Avoiding conflicts Being left alone
For Mother, Happiness was:	A clean house Obedient children Not being contradicted

My parents slept in separate rooms, and I grew up in a tense, silent, "cold war" environment. As with many poor families, it was impossible to educate all the children. I was the third child and the only boy. Quebec in the 1940s and '50s was a very white and Catholic province. For many families, it was an honor to have a son go into the priesthood. It was also a way for children to get a higher education.

With the help and financial assistance of our parish, I was sent as an innocent altar boy to Externat Classique Sainte Croix seminary, where I was going to be trained to become a priest.

Instead, my life changed there. I was sexually abused by one of the priests/professors. The experience shattered my innocence, my faith, and my trust in God. I felt trapped. I could not say anything to my parents. In their eyes, a priest is God; therefore, he could do no wrong. I internalized the abuse as: *I am bad. I am a sinner. I will go to Hell.*

When the abuse continued, I complained to Father Superior. I was promised that the abuser would be sent away to another school. Instead, I was sent to Seminaire Marie Mediatrice. It was a time of inner turmoil and inner conflicts. In my case, sexual abuse resulted in sexual addiction. My imprints regarding sex were:

- *Sex is a sin: it's bad, it's dirty, and I am bad and dirty so I will go to Hell.*

- *Sex is forbidden and hidden (even my parents did not sleep together).*

- *Sex is only possible if you masturbate or have sex with prostitutes.*

- *I have no right to sexual boundaries.*

Needless to say, these imprints made it necessary for me to numb my guilt and shame whenever I was sexually active. I began numbing the pain with alcohol. I already had the genetic predisposition to alcoholism, but the shame regarding my sexuality and sexual abuse was the trigger for both addictions to co-exist; together, they created for me a life of guilt, shame, hidden acting out, and self-rejection. For years, I went from one relationship to another, as the saying goes, "Looking for love in all the wrong places." The result was a few divorces that added to my burden of guilt, shame, and self-rejection.

I entered recovery when I was thirty years old, without knowing that my imprints kept on controlling my life. In my first ten years of sobriety, I rebuilt my career as an interior designer. I proved to others and myself that I was not a charity case, but a successful and creative man; I even had my own TV show on interior design. I was considered a "winner" in terms of all the material stuff our society views as necessary to be successful. Yet my heart felt empty, restless. I needed more.

After ten years of sobriety, I changed my career and started working in the field of alcoholism. By then, I knew that service was my calling. Helping others was part of my childhood dream to serve God.

What I did not know then was that unless we resolve and remove our negative imprints, they continue to be the addictive triggers to our self-defeating behaviors.

At fifteen years of abstinence from alcohol, due to my unresolved sexual and relational imprints, I developed a chemical dependence on prescription medication. It almost cost me my marriage and my new career. It was the wakeup call I needed for my transformation.

Looking back at my life, I am still amazed at my transformation. My imprints have been changed and the script of my life has been re-written. I am forty-five years sober from alcohol, and thirty years sober from any mood altering substance. I quit smoking ten years ago. I have been in recovery for my sexual addiction for the past twenty-seven years. I have been working for the past thirty-four years of my life in the field of addictions.

I am happily married to my soulmate, best friend, business partner, and fellow in recovery for the past thirty-one years. Our communications are based on mutual respect, trust, openness, honesty, and humility. We share passion and tenderness, prayers and spiritual belief systems. Together, we share daily our gratitude lists for all the blessings big and small. My life is an open book without any hidden agendas.

I am no more a charity case. I am a prosperous man: I have loving family relationships, beautiful friendships, and a happy marriage. I am healthy. I am financially stable, and I am responsible, generous, and prosperous. A great positive imprint I received from my dad is the respect and joy found in a good day's work.

My imprint that English-speaking people have the power has been rewritten too. When we closed the French Pavillon, I had to start working in English. I had no clue how I was going to do that. I had to learn. Well, for the past twenty-six years, I have been working in English with people from all over Canada, the United States, and the world. My dad used to be so impressed by English-speaking Canadians, so he must be really impressed by my transformation. We did it Dad. That one is for you!

I rewrote many other imprints for both dad and me. My dad loved baseball so much. Every time I watch a game on my big color TV screen, I think of you, Dad; you would have been so impressed and happy to see the game so close and clear on a big screen.

My imprint of love has changed too. Love is not only providing and avoiding problems and responsibilities. Love is being present and being safe for others. Love is listening and sharing. Love is enjoying playing golf with my wife, without keeping score, and without wanting to be elsewhere. Love is taking risks. Love is trusting God, others, and myself. Love is forgiving, accepting, and allowing others to be. Love is truly being whom I was meant to be. Love is the peace I have in my heart. Love is the joy I experience when I play with our little dog Angel.

Sex and my sexuality are no longer triggers of shame and guilt. I have reclaimed my innocence and dignity. From believing sex is a sin, I have come a long way. My new imprint is that sex is a communication system. Making love is a spiritual, mental, emotional, and sexual Communion. To me, that is freedom.

My relationship with God has undergone a 180-degree transformation. In place of my childhood imprint of the distant judge up in the sky who abandoned me, I now have an intimate and personal relationship with God. I know my true origin and my essence. I know that my main purpose on this planet is to love and to be a better man each day. I know that truly to love, I need daily to surrender the ego and embrace my Identity. For that I am truly grateful. I love my life and all the people in it. And yes I am free.

* * *

I am grateful to my husband for his willingness to share his story. A marriage and a relationship are like a garden. They require tender loving care. In the past thirty-one years of our marriage, Gilles and I have gone through rocky days, scary days, and days of triumphs and celebration.

When my husband and I committed to letting go of negative imprints and ego, our purpose and mission as a couple were revealed. Working as business partners together has been an adventure in the dance of boundaries. We had to rewrite old scripts of codependent enmeshments to create an empowering, synergistic partnership.

We had to learn not to cater to each other's needs according to our own. When I am tired and/or afraid, my need is: be with me, hold me, talk to me. When my husband is tired and/or afraid his need is: leave me alone, don't question me, don't interrogate me, let me figure it out. My husband used to cater to my need according to his own, by leaving me alone, which would than add rejection and abandonment to my fatigue or fear.

I used to cater to his needs according to mine, and when he would be tired and/or afraid I would question him, hold him, touch him, pushing him to share and get it off his chest—the "let's talk" theory—which made him feel like he was suffocating and being controlled.

We both had to rewrite a big imprint that said: *Assume that you know what the other needs.* Instead we learned to listen and learn from each other by asking simple questions: What would be helpful to you now? Can I do something for you? We allowed each other to express our needs. My imprint said: *I have to resolve "their" problem because I am responsible for "their" feelings.* My husband's imprint said: *"Don't rock the boat ...leave!"*

Growing up, neither of us had ever seen a healthy and creative resolution of conflict nor viewed an example of how to set healthy boundaries. But now we took personal responsibility for our needs, boundaries, and the communication of those to our partner.

Today, we have a Golden Rule. In time of conflict, we take time out. We go individually into our space to identify the exact nature of *our* wrongs. We both have a lot of experience in knowing our partner's wrongs. However, it is when I identify which of my old imprints has crept in and is triggering old reactive behavioral patterns that I regain my freedom. I am the only person I can change. When we come back, we share the exact nature of our wrongs. This removes the emotional charge and we resolve the issue at hand easily and quickly.

When we give our Sacred Yes to a creative, organic partnership with God/Higher Power (or whatever we call our Creator), we will be stretched and projected out of our comfort zones.

15 The Spiritual Dimension

The Power of Prayer and Meditation

We use to dream of our "golden years" and retirement. Well, our retirement started on a rough road for many reasons, some due to old imprints of "Them vs. Us." However, the big shock came three months into our retirement. We were just returning from a trip to the Dominican Republic and Puerto Rico. My husband started feeling ill in the Dominican Republic, and things got much worse in San Juan. The flight back home to North Carolina was the longest flight of my life.

The next morning, my husband went to see his doctor, who immediately sent him to see a cardiologist. Within the next five days, our lives were turned upside down. Gilles had to have quadruple bypass surgery due to blocked arteries.

On the night before surgery, Gilles did not want to spend the evening in our hotel room, so we went for dinner and to see the movie *Chicago*. The dinner and the movie were heavy because we were worried about what would happen the next day. When we came back to the hotel room, both of us were vulnerable. We could not make love; Gilles was having difficulty breathing; however, we still expressed love for each other. We talked about our fears of losing each other, and together, we surrendered our fears. We shared the longest moment of intimacy and vulnerability together as we expressed to each other our love and our gratitude for the years of magic we had created together. It was a time of deep tenderness and oneness. It was a time of faith, hope, and trust. We did not know whether we were going to see each other again, yet both of us had hearts filled with so much awe and gratitude for whom we were together and for what we had shared for so many years.

The next day, I took my best friend to the surgery department, and then with family and friends, I spent the longest day of my life. The surgery was scheduled before noon, yet we did not see the surgeon until 5:30 that afternoon. Gilles was alive! The surgeon told us he had done a great job with the arteries; however, the next forty-eight hours would be critical because of Gilles' enlarged and weakened heart.

The power of prayer to heal has been studied, debated, denied, and documented. While I have great respect for scientific research, I have to tell you that ever since my near-death experience, I trust my intuition, and I know the role our minds play in healing. I have personally experienced it.

In *Holistic Health Magazine*, Dennis Hughes interviewed Larry Dossey, MD, and author of *Reinventing Medicine: Beyond Mind-Body to a New Era of Healing*. Here is what Dr. Dossey said about the three eras of healing:

> Era One began in the 1850s, 1860s. Today we call this mechanical medicine. It's the use of drugs, surgical procedures, radiation and so forth. And it's obviously still with us; it dominates medicine. But beginning in 1950, or thereabouts, a new era began which I call Era Two. Today this is known as mind and body medicine. It used to be called psychosomatic disease. Basically, it's the idea that our emotions and thoughts, and feelings can affect health. Era Three includes the ability of consciousness to reach out beyond ourselves to make a difference in other people. Intercessory prayer is an example of an era three therapy—healing intention.

During the forty-eight hours following my husband's surgery, there was an international circle of prayers going my husband's way. I don't mean just a few individuals. I am talking about people from around the world who loved my husband. Some were praying for his recovery because he helped them change their lives. Some were praying because they were his family members. Some were praying because they were his fellows in recovery. Some were praying because they were members of his spiritual family. Some were saying Jewish prayers, some were saying Catholic prayers, some were praying in a variety of Christian churches, some were praying Muslim prayers. Some could only say the Serenity prayer and some were "not praying" but sending him positive and affirmative thoughts, and some were meditating sending the sound of "Om," and sending him Light, the healing white light.

The form of prayer did not matter; we were all sending him *love*. The healing energy of love. Gilles was receptive and responsive to it. My husband's heart regained 100 percent of its capacity. He fully recovered. Three months later, when we went to see the cardiologist, he said to my husband, "Mr. Desjardins, your recovery is phenomenal. You are doing great. If it would not be for the ethics, I would give you a hug." To which my husband said, "Doctor, let's forget about the ethics and just give me the hug." He did. With tears in his eyes, my husband thanked the doctor for saving his life. Dr. Jenkins looked at both of us and said, "I did a good job; the surgeon did a great job. You did your part Mr. Desjardins, but we all know who is the true healer."

Wow! That is humility. It was a team effort! The phrase "With God all things are possible" suddenly had a deeper meaning. Call it God, Jesus, the Holy Spirit,

Allah, Buddha, Light, Universe, The Field—the terminology does not matter! The best of the three eras of healing that Dr. Dossey talks about were applied with remarkable result.

Gilles' recovery was phenomenal for another reason: he did his post-surgery recovery with Tylenol only. He had eight cuts on his legs and a big scar on his chest. Due to his past chemical dependency, painkillers were not an option. We walked together through the pain. It was meditation instead of medication. The overall results were long lasting. My husband totally changed his eating habits. He developed a dietary discipline. I did not have to be the food police; my husband became aware, responsible, and accountable for his own nutrition. The gym got a new regular member. Dr. Jenkins told us that 50 percent of patients come back for the same procedure because they do not change their lifestyles. Gilles did not want to be part of that 50 percent. He took charge of his wellbeing, thereby reducing his healthcare costs. The entire process was a joint healing process.

The time Gilles invested in meditation not only alleviated his physical pain, but it healed the wounds and scars of his grieving heart. As one of the volunteers at the hospital said, "Mr. Desjardins, you have a new heart."

Meditation is a powerful healing tool. Herbert Vincent has spent twenty years at Harvard University studying meditation. His research shows that meditative states, and almost any kind of contemplative state, can be good for the body. When people meditate, their blood pressure goes down, the heart rate falls, and immune changes take place in the body.

The science is irrefutable; more than 340 studies on the benefits of meditation have been published in top scientific journals. The National Institute of Health, the American Medical Association, and the American Heart Association have all funded or published Transcendental Meditation research for decades.

Meditation is such a powerful tool to reduce and change so many health problems as well as socio-economic problems our society faces. *It is free, yet due to old imprints, it is so underused!*

From Breakdown to Breakthrough

We live in an addicted society. We live in a time of school bullying, teenage suicides, poor test results, and overcrowded schools. Metal detectors and security guards are protecting our children in our schools from gang wars. Obesity, type-2 diabetes, heart disease, and related diseases fill our hospitals. Our Iraq and Afghanistan veterans suffer from post-traumatic stress disorder. Our prisons are overcrowded with people incarcerated for drug possession or drug-related charges. The war on drugs goes on in spite of its failure. Our prison guards are stressed out from the pressure-cookers behind thick walls. Our streets are filled with the homeless.

Americans live in the most powerful and "successful" country in the world, yet we are a highly stressed and highly medicated nation. Our children are medicated and on Ritalin. They are abused by the fast food and high fat/high sugar diets fed to them in our schools and homes.

Children are the future of any nation. Why do we abuse them? Why have we created such social messes? Is it because of our governing systems in place? Is it because of greed and corruption? Or is it because of negative imprints passed from one generation to the next which feed the greed and corruption?

In my life, I have lived under fascism and the atrocities it produced. I have lived under communism, where the state nationalized all for which my parents worked. I have lived under socialism, where the state provided free education and healthcare and all the problems that went with trying to provide for everyone. I have lived and am living under capitalism. I know the benefits and downfalls of all of them. I have seen all of them fail.

What is Fascism? Fascism is a political theory advocating an authoritarian hierarchical government (as opposed to Democracy or Liberalism).

What is Communism? Communism is state capitalism, in which all or most means of production are owned and controlled by "the state," and few or no means of production are owned and controlled by individuals.

What is Socialism? The term "Socialism" properly refers to any economic system, whether capitalistic or "laboristic," that adopts as its objective the greatest economic good for the greatest number. Experience makes it clear that this requires dispersing the ownership and control of the means of production as widely as possible.

What is Capitalism? Any economy that derives most of its production from the employment of Capital may be said to be capitalism. There is no true "opposite" of capitalism, but capitalism stands in most direct contrast with "laborism" or economies that derive most of their production from human labor. In practice, there are no economies that are purely capitalistic or "laboristic."

The form of capitalism practiced in the United States is Economic Elitism, or the degenerate economic conservatism, which is any economic system that seeks maximum good for a tiny elite at the expense of majority.

We can blame governments, yet we elect them. We can blame corporations, yet we buy their products. We can blame the biggest legal pushers of drugs: the pharmaceutical companies who spend billions of dollars selling us medication for anything imaginable. Through grants given to our universities, they rule the research and write the Diagnostic and Statistical Manual of Mental Health Disorders, yet we want instant solutions and magical pills for our Addiction to Suffering.

We can blame the media for selling all these products. We can blame the media for irresponsible, biased, and dishonest reporting, yet we continue to watch its programming. We can blame the media for being owned by the same economic elitism that runs the country, sacrificing integrity journalism for ratings...yet we buy it, and we believe it. The media is but the reflection of our Security Addiction and Power Control Addiction. The more antagonistic, violent, aggressive, or frightening movies and programs are, the better they sell...because we buy them.

The "Joe Six-Pack" is not a rumor but a true mentality; Joe Six-Pack is not just a Republican, a Democrat, or an Independent. Joe Six-Pack is the Sensation Addiction in reality. We can blame political and religious fanaticism, yet we perpetuate both of them. Does that mean we need to blame ourselves?

What it all really means is that if as a species we intend to survive, we need to wake up before it is too late. The blame game is part of the same imprint that got us into this mess. What we need to change are our imprints and belief systems.

We can have elections, changes of governments and systems, yet nothing will change until we change the very imprints that have produced dysfunction and continue to perpetuate that dysfunction. We have to change our collective imprints and consciousness. We cannot operate on old beliefs any longer.

As I said in the beginning of this book, it is a paradoxical world. *My change must start with me.* When our focus is on change and possibilities, we start discovering a new world. Lately, I have come across so many fantastic articles, stories, and projects that show me so much good is happening on this planet...but good does not make the same kind of noise as dysfunction.

One positive example of good on this planet is the David Lynch Foundation for consciousness-based education and world peace. It is transforming lives by providing funds for students to learn to meditate through TM teaching centers, hospital-sponsored wellness programs, boys and girls clubs, before and after-school programs, and in schools when invited by the administration. Instruction is voluntary and is provided to a child with the permission of a parent at no cost to the family, school, or organization. In the past year, the David Lynch Foundation has provided millions of dollars to teach thousands of students, teachers, and parents how to meditate. The Foundation also provides funds for independent research institutions to assess the effects of the program on creativity, intelligence, brain functioning, academic performance, ADHD, and other learning disorders, anxiety, depression, and substance abuse.

Plus, the Foundation has made a great effort to help at-risk populations that suffer from epidemic levels of chronic stress and stress-related disorders, thus fueling violence, crime, and soaring healthcare costs, and compromising the effectiveness of educational, rehabilitation, and vocational programs now in place. To counter these problems, the David Lynch Foundation gives millions of dollars for the implementation of scientifically proven stress-reducing modalities, including TM. Among the at-risk populations it serves are underserved inner-city students; Native Americans suffering from diabetes, cardiovascular disease, and high suicide rates; Iraq and Afghanistan veterans suffering from PTSD; homeless men participating in re-entry programs and striving to overcome addictions; and incarcerated juveniles and adults.

One foundation doing a lot of good to bring about necessary change!

Imagine the Change. The interest in Transcendental Meditation (TM) has reached a level that might not have been possible in the 1960s when the Beatles first hit the music scene, but in April 2009, Paul McCartney and Ringo Starr headlined a "Change Begins Within" concert at Radio City Music Hall with the intention of raising enough money to teach meditation techniques to children on every continent. It was a celebration of consciousness creativity and bliss, with participation by Russell Simmons, Sheryl Crow, and many other well-known performers. Sounds too good to be true—like a line from the old John Lennon song "Imagine."

Another remarkable institution doing great work and good on the planet is The Institute of Noetic Sciences (IONS). The institute was founded in 1973 by Apollo astronaut Edgar Mitchell. It is a nonprofit research, education, and membership organization whose mission is advancing the science of consciousness and human experience to serve individual and collective transformation. Noetic comes from the Greek word *nous*, which means "intuitive mind" or "inner knowing." IONS conducts, sponsors, and collaborates on leading-edge research into the potentials and powers of consciousness, exploring phenomena that do not necessarily fit conventional scientific models while maintaining a commitment to scientific rigor. The institute's primary program areas are consciousness and healing, extended human capacities, and emerging worldviews.

The Institute of HeartMath Research Center in California is another recognized global leader in emotional physiology and stress-management research. HeartMath is engaged in basic psychophysiology, neurocardiology and biophysics research, as well as clinical, workplace, and organizational intervention and treatment outcome studies in collaboration with numerous universities, research centers, and healthcare-system partners. This research has significantly advanced the understanding of heart-brain interaction.

The heart-brain interaction is greatly impaired by negative imprints.

HeartMath's website www.HeartMath.com publishes some of its research and one study of major interest is its Global Coherence Research as stated on its website:

> HeartMath Institute Is Involved in Global Coherence Research
>
> There is a growing sense around the world that we live in times of great change and upheaval, relative not only to the physical integrity of our planet and atmosphere—because of stewardship of the space we inhibit has reached a point of "incoherence"—but also to human beings, who increasingly are rejecting an existence whose credo is "get ahead at any cost"—the price of which is a uniquely modern malaise of pandemic

stress and fear, global strife and planetary decay, and personal and collective sadness.

As we can see, globally the old imprints do not work any longer. It is time for change.

> The Institute of HeartMath and its research team, already in the forefront of stress-management research, are on a quest to foster global coherence by going beyond what we already know about heart-brain interaction, heart intelligence and heart coherence. We want to be a leader in service to humankind as the paradigm shift of our time unfolds and people in every nation begin reconnecting with their hearts, turning away from stressful and self-centered living and turning toward heart-based living and global coherence.

All this great research is pointing us in the right direction. Yes, change is happening all around us. Old paradigms do not work any longer. Order emerges out of chaos. Systems need to break down before we can experience the breakthroughs. We need to die to the old ideas and old imprints for the new to be born. Globally we are in a time where our imaginal cells are being activated but the ego cells are still attacking them, fighting for the old status quo.

Life is about Change

In life, one thing is constant and consistent—change. Life is about change, growth, and evolution. My life is a testimony to the power of change and re-invention.

In this book, I wanted so much to talk about my and our children, but out of respect for their privacy I chose not to. Beyond the shadow of a doubt, they are the greatest gifts life has given me, and I am so profoundly grateful for all the love, joy, beauty, greatness, and teachings they have brought into my life. I deeply admire who they are and what they do. Our bond, our love, and the quality of our relationship is a testimony to the Power of Forgiveness and the Power of Love. I am so grateful for their courage, integrity, vision, and commitment to make the world a better place. Together we have rewritten the script of family imprints and our joint legacy is health, sanity, and love. A gift that keeps on giving.

For reasons of privacy, I did not talk about the twelve years we lived in North Carolina, nor our involvement at Pavillon International. Building the facility and operating the facility has been an incredible experience and growth process. We will forever be grateful to all the individuals concerned who were involved in the project. It was a great team effort. At times, it was like the song says, "running against the wind" and at other times we really felt the "wind beneath our wings." Forever we will keep fond memories of joint victories and dreams that came true.

Before our move to Texas, we had the chance to express our gratitude to the staff, the board, the suppliers, the neighbors, as well as the clients. Once again *thank you* for having enriched our lives by your presence.

As I said, life is about change. Pavillon International in Mill Spring, North Carolina has changed and has a new mission. It is a beautiful facility in an inspiring environment where substance addictions are professionally treated.

The Desjardins Unified Model for Inpatient Treatment of Addictions does not exist any longer. Out of it has emerged a powerful new model, which focuses on the healing of imprints and allows individuals with or without substance issues truly to transform their lives. This inpatient model is at Chatsworth Pavillon in Montreal, Canada*.

Chatsworth's philosophy is that repetitive self-defeating patterns, dependencies, and addictions represent an exaggerated need to self-medicate that is anchored in learned negative imprints as well as genetic imprints. Until the emotional imprints are addressed, even if one stops their primary self-medicating strategy, others will appear. Chatsworth's Model empowers individuals to embrace their Identity and tap into their Authentic Self, thus transforming weaknesses into strengths, negative self-esteem into self-worth and confidence. It truly helps turn the dependency into autonomy and isolation into communication.

This inpatient model produces the acceleration of the transformational process Dr. Hawkins talks about. It empowers the shift from the low calibrating emotional energies into the higher energy levels. Lower energies being: shame which calibrates at level 20, and is the closest to death; guilt at energy level 30; grief at energy level 75, fear at 100, and anger calibrating at 150. By removing the negative imprints these lower energies get shifted into the higher energies of courage calibrating at 200, willingness calibrating at 310, acceptance calibrating at 350, and love calibrating at 500.

This closed model becomes the cocoon of transformation allowing the imaginal cells of each individual to awaken, thus tapping into their creative genius within. It becomes a process of consciousness building.

Great changes are happening on our planet! Imagine our contribution to the wellbeing of the planet when we decide to tap into our Authentic Self, our true Identity. Imagine the quality of our lives when we become aware of whom we truly are, and we change our belief systems as the Action Steps to Transformation described in this book teach us. Imagine how powerful we become when our Imprints are Abundance, Empowerment and Manageability, Enjoyment and Creativity. Imagine the quality of relationships we will experience when these positive imprints determine the quality of our lives.

Imagine the positive role models we become when we make this transformation. Since Transcendental Meditation works while we are sitting on top of our negative

---

* www.chatsworthpavilion.com, tollfree 866-931-2999.

imprints, imagine the Power of Creativity we have when our negative imprints are identified, processed, changed and then, through meditation, we access our greatness and fulfill the true purpose of our lives.

Our minds and hearts, when connected to the Universal Energy and our Creator, are the most potent Power in the Universe. It is our responsibility and ability to tap into that power. The Global Heart on our planet is awakening; all the recent tsunamis and earthquakes have demonstrated that we have global compassion.

I know for a fact that thousands have already joined me on this journey. I personally know many who have chosen to be co-creators with Life/God/Love/the Universe and whose lives have been transformed as a result.

Years ago, I would have had a hard time believing that life can be transformed, that all relationships can be healed. Years ago, I could not imagine that my parents would spend the last years of their lives living with us in peace and harmony, and that I would have the opportunity to rewrite the script of our relationships and imprints from one of pain into one of love, tenderness, and gentle care. After all, my parents used to be the greatest triggers for my ego. But as has been demonstrated, with God all things are possible.

The day of my suicide attempt, I did not think that one day I would be a licensed clinical addiction specialist or that our program would become the success it did, helping thousands to transform their lives.

When I was in the process of dealing with my inadequacies, shame and guilt, I did not think that someday I would write a book about all of it, free from pain of the past and amazed at the miracles and blessings in my life and the lives of people around me.

In my wildest dreams, I could not have imagined being married to my soul-mate, best friend, life partner, and business partner for thirty-one years and still be in love as at the beginning. WOW! I did not think that every year we were going to reinvent ourselves by establishing a clear vision of who we wanted to be and a clear vision of our mission. I am so grateful. Like my friend Ernie Larson used to say, "Healthy relationships require two willing and capable people." Many are willing, and once negative imprints are removed, they become capable.

When we do the inner work and we embrace our Identity, deep transformation follows. In my case, it was a deep inner reconciliation with all religions and all nations, followed by a sense of oneness. I was able to transcend our diversities and marvel at our commonalities. Having traveled a great portion of our world, I am amazed by how in our hearts we all aspire to the same values, needs, and desires.

In 2004, my husband and I took my step-mom to Croatia. I was amazed there by the resilience of the people after the war of 1990. They are back on their feet again, better than ever. When we went to Bosnia and saw the devastation, my heart was with my Muslim Compatriots. I am so happy to be part of the program Women for Women International because it gives me a chance to sponsor women from Bosnia. On our way to Croatia, we stopped in Germany and I experienced the depth of my forgiveness and understanding. I was capable of looking into the German people's beautiful blue eyes and seeing past the time of horror and shame in our history.

Yes, transformation and healings are possible because our Authentic Self is Whole and well. When we remove the erroneously programmed negative imprints, our Co-Creator's wisdom shines. The twenty-first century requires all of us to grow up. The world is filled with "Children of God." Now is the time for us to grow up and show up. It is time to take responsibility for our greatness and to be the Co-Creators we were meant to be.

I am very grateful to you for having been a faithful reader to the end of this book. More than that, I want to thank you for being willing to change, to grow, and to believe in yourself. Our transformation is the greatest gift we can give our children.

To all of you who, in the past thirty-six years, have traveled with me down the road less traveled, thank you for being consciousness builders. Together we are building the critical mass that produces paradigm shifts on this planet.

When I started writing this book, my desire was to be true to myself, to be open, receptive, and obedient to my Intuition and Inner Guidance. I have been true. Now my desire is for you to be inspired and to be guided to Transform your pain into Triumph for yourself and others.

Appendix: Imprints Worksheet for Your Own Imprint Journey

Key imprints areas:

- Love/relationships/family/extended family
- Health / body / sexuality
- Financial
- Religious/spiritual
- Educational
- Social
- Life's purpose/success

Core questions to ask yourself in order to identify an imprint regarding the above key areas:

- What is the negative and positive role modeling I have received growing up (regarding the key areas)
- What were the negative and positive (spoken and unspoken) messages I have received growing up from:
  - Family
  - Educators
  - Religion
  - Society
- How have I internalized these messages
- What is my deep seated belief, perception and feeling regarding the role modeling and messages I have received in the above key areas
- Is it a belief that was carried over from one generation to the other
- Which of my behaviors are still triggered or affected by this belief/ perception
- What difficulties is my belief/perception still causing in my life
- Is the difficulty persisting in spite of different efforts to change it

Introspective work instructions

Choose one key area to work on , take the most problematic one to get the best results! When your choice is made, here are the subquestions you can ask yourself about this key area:

[Example: *What kind of a relationship do I have with money?*]

- What kind of a relationship do I have with _____?
- Do I struggle with it?   How and why?
- Do I feel worth of it? If yes why?
- Do I feel unworthy of it? If yes why?
- How do I perceive _____?
- What is my deep seated belief about it?
- How did I acquire this belief?
- How does my belief about _____ make me behave?
- What are the negative messages and role modeling I have received in my childhood regarding _____?
- How did my father handle _____?
- What kind of a relationship did he have with _____?
- How did my mother handle _____?
- What kind of a relationship did she have with _____?
- What were the messages I have received from religion regarding _____?
- What were the messages I have received from my educators regarding _____?
- What were the messages I have received from society and media regarding _____?
- What do I believe my imprint about _____ is:
- What are the positive messages and role modeling I have received regarding _____?
- If I would allow your authentic self/co-creator to reveal to me the truth about _____ what would that be?

About the Author

Liliane Desjardins was born in Zagreb, Croatia and educated in Paris, France. Her background is liturgical arts, and among her outstanding works are the Stained Glass windows at the Catholic Chapel at Kennedy International Airport in New York. Upon entering recovery from addictions, Liliane's focus shifted from aesthetic beauty to reshaping and re-creating her life and the lives of others.

Liliane is a Certified Clinical Addiction Specialist. She is renowned for her highly successful and innovative work and the Desjardins Unified Model of Treatment of Addictions. She is the co-founder of Pavillon Gilles Desjardins in Val David, Quebec, Canada and Pavillon International, a center for treatment of addictions in North Carolina. She has thirty-two years of experience in clinical work.

Liliane has a profound and passionate dedication to her work, which is rooted in thirty-six years of personal recovery. Liliane is a proven leader in the healing of emotions and deep-seated self-defeating belief systems and imprints. She has brought hope and healing to thousands. She is an international speaker, workshop leader, and has appeared on numerous educational television programs. She co-authored the book *Rewriting Life Scripts: Transformational Recovery for Families of Addicts*.

With humor, expertise, and compassion, Liliane creates the necessary elements for transformation, as well as the desire and strength needed for individuals to change and lead more effective and healthy lives.

After retiring from Pavillon, Liliane and her husband Gilles moved to Austin, Texas. Liliane is president of Higher Power Productions and conducts monthly four-day programs. Her focus is now on empowering individuals to access their Authentic Self, actualize their potential, and gain freedom from fear-based imprints.

Liliane enjoys playing golf with her husband Gilles and playing with their adorable little dog named Angel.

Bibliography

Beckwith, M. B. (2008). *Spiritual liberation: Fulfilling your soul's potential*. New York: Atria Books/Beyond Words.

Beyondananda, ., & Bhaerman, S. (1989). *Driving your own Karma: Swami Beyondananda's tour guide to enlightenment*. Rochester, Vt: Destiny Books.

Boland, J. (1992). *Master mind goal achiever's journal*. Warren, Mich: Master Mind Pub. Co.

Carnes, P., & Moriarity, J. (1997). *Sexual anorexia: Overcoming sexual self-hatred*. Center City, Minn: Hazelden.

Desjardins, L., Oelklaus, N., & Watson, I. (2009). *Rewriting life scripts: Transformational recovery for families of addicts*. Ann Arbor, MI: Life Scripts Press.

Dossey, L. (1999). *Reinventing medicine: Beyond mind-body to a new era of healing*. San Francisco: Harper SanFrancisco.

Dyer, W. W. (2004). *The power of intention: Learning to co-create your world your way*. Carlsbad, Calif: Hay House.

Fox, M. (1983). *Original blessing*. Santa Fe, N.M: Bear.

Frankl, V. E., Frankl, V. E., Frankl, V. E., Gardner, G., Recorded Books, Inc., & NetLibrary, Inc. (2008). *Man's search for ultimate meaning*. Your coach in a box. Prince Frederick, MD: Recorded Books.

Fromm, E. (1971). *The Crisis of psychoanalysis: Eric Fromm*. London: J. Cape.

Foundation for Inner Peace. (1975). *A course in miracles*. s.l.: Foundation for Inner Peace.

Hawkins, D. R. (2009). *Healing and recovery*. W. Sedona, Ariz: Veritas Pub.

Hawkins, D. R. (2002). *Power vs. force: The hidden determinants of human behavior*. Carlsbad, Calif: Hay House.

Holliwell, R. N. (2004). *Working with the law*. Camarillo, Calif: DeVorss Publications.

Holmes, E. (1928). *The science of mind; a complete course of lessons in the science of mind and spirit*. New York: R.M. McBride & Co.

Huddle, N., Kikuchi, Y., Hayashi, Y., Hayashi, N., & Imamura, K. (2002). *Batafurai =: Butterfly : Idai na hen'yō no chiisana monogatari ; Moshi chikyū ga chō ni nattara*.

Jung, C. G. (1969). *On the nature of the psyche*. Princeton, N.J: Princeton University Press.

Jung, C. G. (1973). *Synchronicity: An acausal connecting principle*. Princeton, N.J.: Princeton University Press.

Keyes, K. S. (1973). *Handbook to higher consciousness: 4th ed.* Berkeley, Calif: Living Love Center.

Lewis, T., Amini, F., & Lannon, R. (2000). *A general theory of love.* New York: Random House.

Lipton, B. H. (2008). *The biology of belief: Unleashing the power of consciousness, matter & miracles.* Carlsbad, Calif: Hay House.

McTaggart, L. (2002). *The field: The quest for the secret force of the universe.* New York, NY: HarperCollins.

Murphy, J., & Pell, A. R. (2009). *Putting the power of your subconscious mind to work: Reach new levels of career success using the power of your subconscious mind.* New York: Prentice Hall Press.

Nu'aymah, M. (1974). *The book of Mirdad: A lighthouse and a haven.* London: Watkins.

Orloff, J. (2009). *Emotional freedom: Liberate yourself from negative emotions and transform your life.* New York: Harmony Books.

Rutledge, T. (2003, December 08). Don't start a war just because you don't feel at peace. *Counterpunch,* Retrieved from http://www.counterpunch.org/rutledge12082003.html

Satir, V. (1972). *Peoplemaking.* Palo Alto, Calif: Science and Behavior Books.

Teilhard, . C. P. (1959). *The phenomenon of man.* New York: Harper.

Index

Rewriting Life Scripts
Transformational Recovery
for Families of Addicts

by
Nancy Oelklaus
Irene Watson
Liliane Desjardins

PRAISE

*A*n invaluable roadmap
for anyone navigating the
difficult journey through
the family disease of alcoholism, with
stories of success from real people
who have 'been there, done that' and
are willing to share their experience,
strength and hope. Addiction doesn't
discriminate and neither should
recovery—recovery for the family too.

William C. Moyers
author of Broken and a New Day,
A New Life: A Guided Journal

MORE INFORMATION

Find more information about the book and the authors at
http://www.higherpowerfoundation.com/about-book/

www.HigherPowerFoundation.com/about-book

CPSIA information can be obtained at www.ICGtesting.com
Printed in the USA
LVOW130313261011

252013LV00002B/1/P

Intermediate Italian For Dummies®

Cheat Sheet

Definite, Indefinite, and Partitive Articles

In Italian, articles vary in gender, number, spelling. They're the best predictor of a noun's gender. The following table outlines the three types of articles and their variations.

Gender/Number	Definite (the)	Indefinite (a, an)	Partitive (a little, some, any)
masculine singular	il, lo, l'	uno, un	del, dello, dell'
feminine singular	la, l'	una, un',	della, dell'
masculine plural	i, gli	—	dei, degli
feminine plural	le	—	delle

Personal Pronouns

Personal pronouns in Italian serve the same purpose as in English. Italian has some pronouns that English doesn't have though — stressed and double pronouns.

Person/ Number	Subject Pronouns	Direct Object Pronouns	Indirect Object Pronouns	Stressed Pronouns	Reflexive Pronouns	Double Pronouns
1/S	io	mi	mi	me	mi	me lo/la/ li/le
2/S (informal)	tu	ti	ti	te	ti	te lo/la/ li/le
3/S	lui/lei	lo/la	gli/le	lui/lei	si	glielo/-la/ -li/-le
2/S (formal)	Lei	La	Le	Lei	Si	Glielo/ -la/-li/-le
1/P	noi	ci	ci	noi	ci	ce lo/la/ li/le
2/P (informal)	voi	vi	vi	voi	vi	ve lo/ la/li/le
3/P (informal)	loro	li/le	gli	loro	si	glielo/ -la/-li/-le
2/P (formal)	Loro	Li/Le	—	Loro	Si	

Simple Prepositions

Italian has eight basic prepositions, which correspond to the basic prepositions used in English. Remember, though, that although the translations shown here reflect the meanings in the two languages, the usage sometimes differs between the two languages, depending on context. See Chapter 6 for details. The basic prepositions are as follows:

- **di** (*of, about*)
- **a** (*at, to*)
- **da** (*from, by*)
- **con** (*with*)
- **in** (*in, into*)
- **su** (*on, onto*)
- **per** (*for, through*)
- **fra/tra** (*between, among*)

For Dummies: Bestselling Book Series for Beginners

Intermediate Italian For Dummies®

Italian/English Mood and Tense Equivalences

This section provides you with an at-a-glance view of the various moods and tenses Italian verbs can take.

Modo Indicativo (Indicative Mood)

Tense	Example
presente (*simple present*)	**io guardo** (*I look*)
presente progressivo (*present progressive*)	**io sto guardando** (*I am looking*)
imperfetto (*imperfect*)	**io guardavo** (*I looked*)
imperfetto progressivo (*past/imperfect progressive*)	**io stavo guardando** (*I was looking*)
passato prossimo (*present perfect*)	**io ho guardato** (*I have looked*)
trapassato prossimo (*past perfect*)	**io avevo guardato** (*I had looked*)
passato remoto (*preterit*)	**io guardai** (*I looked*)
trapassato remoto (*past perfect*)	**io ebbi guardato** (*I had looked*)
futuro (*future*)	**io guarderò** (*I will look*)
futuro anteriore (*future perfect*)	**io avrò guardato** (*I will have looked*)

Modo Congiuntivo (Subjunctive Mood)

Tense	Example
presente (*present*)	**[che] io guardi** (*[that] I look*)
passato (*past*)	**[che] io abbia guardato** (*[that] I have looked*]
imperfetto (*imperfect*)	**[che] io guardassi** (*[that] I looked*)
trapassato (*past perfect*)	**[che] io avessi guardato** (*[that] I had looked*)

Modo Condizionale (Conditional Mood)

Tense	Example
presente (*present*)	**io guarderei** (*I would look*)
passato (*past*)	**io avrei guardato** (*I would have looked*)

Modo Imperative (Imperative Mood)

Tense	Example
presente (*present*)	**guarda!** (*look!*)
futuro (*future*)	**guarderai!** (*add translation*)

Infinito (Infinitive)

Tense	Example
presente (*present*)	**guardare** (*to look*)
passato (*past*)	**avere guardato** (*to have looked*)

Participio (Participle)

Tense	Example
presente (*present*)	**guardante** (*looking*)
futuro (*future*)	**guardato/-a/-i/-e** (*looked*)

Gerundio (Gerund)

Tense	Example
presente (*present*)	**guardando** (*looking*)
futuro (*future*)	**avendo guardato** (*having looked*)